After You've Said I'm Sorry

After You've Said I'm Sorry

Frank Pollard

BROADMAN PRESS
Nashville, Tennessee

For
Ashley Suzanne Pollard
With love from Dad.

4252-02
ISBN: 0-8054-5202-8

Dewey Decimal Classification: 241.3
Subject heading: SIN
Library of Congress Catalog Card Number: 81-70410
Printed in the United States of America

Acknowledgments

Thanks to: Kathy Richardson whose advice and labor were monumental in preparing this work

The loving members of First Baptist Church, San Antonio, Texas, who make me want to communicate God's truth because they want to know it

J. C. Hatfield whose ministry has freed me to pursue my calling, and whose Christian example has inspired me to do so

Brent, my son, who encouraged me to do this

And most of all: to Jane, my wife, my best friend and God's beautiful gift

Foreword

This is for Christian sinners: you who have sinned, begged God for pardon, and soon committed the same sin again. If it is your painful pattern to do wrong, repent it and repeat it, it is your hearing I seek.

Is there a Christian anywhere who does not regretfully remember what it is to sin against God, to be truly sorry and hear him say: "Neither do I condemn you; go your way. From now on sin no more." But the sinful deed was repeated. Haven't all of us, more times than we want to remember, had to go before the throne of God praying: "O Lord, I've done it again!" Soon we honestly ask: "Can nothing be done?" Must one be forever at the mercy of this ruinous repetition of wrong, repentance, and return to wrong?

There is good news!
He will show you the way out.

CONTENTS

1

Gospel!
Romans 1:16

In reference to the thousands of miles he travels each year and the time he must spend away from his family, Billy Graham said: "I would not pay that price for anything in this world except the gospel of Jesus Christ."

One recurring word marks the message of the Bible. That word is *gospel*. When Paul wrote to the people at Rome, he used the word *gospel* to describe the passion of his life and as the common denominator explaining his love for all the world: "For I have complete confidence in the gospel: it is God's power to save all who believe, first the Jews and also the Gentiles" (Rom. 1:16, TEV).

When Billy Graham spoke to the Southern Baptist Convention in Philadelphia, he had just returned from Ireland and was travel weary. He said he felt like the fellow who dreamed he was preaching and woke up to discover he was!

In reference to the hundreds of thousands of miles he travels each year and the time he must spend away from his family, Graham said: "I would not pay that price for anything in this world except the gospel of Jesus Christ."

What is this gospel? It is some facts, but it is much more. It is also a life, a Spirit. The church in the New Testament gives us a good guideline whereby we can check the reality of our own concept of the gospel. What is the gospel of the Lord Jesus Christ? It is a thing to celebrate, a participation in history. It is the heart of Christianity, the hope of Christianity, the invitation of Christianity, and the fellowship of Christians.

One thing is made completely clear by the Bible's description of that beginning band of bold followers of Jesus Christ: The gospel is a thing to celebrate.

The great difference between the church of the first century and the church of the twentieth century is not doctrinal. Both groups believe the same things. The difference is that what they believed about Jesus Christ made them excited, celebrating people.

Celebration does not mean they were constantly partying. It does mean they were spiritually confident. They lived in difficult times. They were poor. In a day of cruelty, violence, superstition, disease, and death, they were celebrating people.

Celebration is no substitute for realism. Yet it does keep reality from driving us to despair. Celebration does not take the place of work. It gives work purpose. Celebration does not exempt people from the routine. It infuses routine with meaning. Celebration does not resist change. It gives it direction. Celebration does not automatically right all the wrongs, but it makes life bearable in the "waiting time."

The gospel begins to reach other people when it is shared by celebrating Christians.

The gospel means knowing that you are involved in what God is doing in history. The early church saw herself as being at the very center of God's action in history. People in the first century knew that Jesus Christ was what God had in mind when he called Abraham. Christ is the fulfilling of hundreds of years of prophecy. When God's time was right, he entered time and history. God was involved in the historical process and is still involved.

We know that to be a part of what Jesus Christ is doing in this day is to be a part of history that is ultimately under God's control. We know that the lasting, meaningful decision will not be made in Washington, DC, nor in Moscow, nor in Peking, but in heaven. We are convinced that as the welfare of the Old Testament world depended upon what God's people did then, the welfare and the destiny of this world depends upon what

God's people do now. The effectual, fervent prayers of a relatively few people committed to Jesus Christ can change the direction of history.

The gospel of Jesus Christ means that God is on the move and those who love him are at the center of that movement. At the very heart of the gospel is the life, death, and resurrection of Jesus Christ. The early church saw the life, death, and resurrection of Jesus Christ as one event. The same Jesus who preached, healed, and lived is the same one who died for our sins and who, because of the resurrection, was a living presence in their lives.

How strange to one-world ears is the intimate prayer of the church whose leaders had just been released from jail with orders not to preach. "And now, Lord, take notice of the threats they made and allow us, your servants, to speak your message with all boldness" (Acts 4:29, TEV).

Those who claim knowledge of the gospel can best prove that by a demonstration of the presence of a living God. The early Christians had absolutely nothing else, but because of his presence they shook the world. It ought to be so today. *Incarnation* means "God with us." The gospel has great power when shared by a people who know God is with them.

When the gospel is shared, there is a preaching of the second coming of Christ. First century Christians greeted each other saying: "The Lord is coming!" When greeted like that, a Christian would smile, a gleam would come to his eye, and he would reply: "The Lord is coming, indeed."

What a shame it is that many believers have become so uptight about our Lord's second coming. Every time I preach on this subject, I expect some chart-carrying theologian to come and tell how he has classified me—like some poor moth captured for a seventh-grade biology class. There are those who would fight a battle fiercer than Armageddon for their interpretation of the last days. Like a dog guarding a precious piece of meat, they snarlingly hover over their concepts, snapping at any passerby who tries to examine what they have. But to the early Christians this was not a battleground of hostility. It was a precious garden of hope.

During Billy Graham's crusade at Madison Square Garden, one of ten sermons he preached was on the second coming. It was a wholesome, straightforward, unapologetic declaration that Jesus Christ is coming back to earth. Many were surprised when they chose that particular sermon as one of three for network television. Several complained about the "utter irrelevance of preaching to troubled urban man about the second coming." Yet large numbers of individuals had responded to Christ after hearing that sermon and had written to Mr. Graham to tell him about their response.

In the television audience were literally millions of persons who had no prejudices about the doctrine. They had not heard the theological hairsplitting on the millennium. To them, the declaration that Jesus Christ was coming again was another way of spelling hope. The early Christians felt the church was not only a part of God's past, but also a part of his future. This hope did not unnerve them. It did not cause them to battle each other. It motivated them to evangelize. They were winners, and they acted like it.

This is a day when the foundations truly shake. People look around them at all that has previously been their basis of security, and everything seems to be coming unglued. This is a day when man desperately needs to hear the word of hope from a people of hope—hope not in ourselves, but in God.

The gospel contains an invitation. Where the gospel is, there is an urgent appeal for people to repent of sin and receive the gift of the Holy Spirit.

In the word *gospel* there is both judgment and healing:

judgment in that we must face up to what we are like; healing in that we discover God loves us even though we are like we are.

Christians learn to see themselves and to see God in a continuing experience. God's ability to accept us has freed us to accept ourselves. It starts us on the road to accepting others. From this a fellowship is born—a fellowship of the accepted and the accepting, of the forgiven and the forgiving, of the loved and the loving. This fellowship is called a church.

The gospel of Jesus Christ is the only ultimate word to mankind. It is a word of celebration. It is filled with history and hope. It is the promise of God with us and also in us. It is a word capable of creating a community that draws its values and its strengths from the same source—God, who reached out to man in Christ.

The Holy Spirit is at work in the whole world. But he also helps one person. He can, will, and wants to help you.

2

Debtor, Not Ashamed, Ready!
Romans 1:14-16

In these three verses are found the daily motivation of Paul's life. You and I can take these statements and make them the mottoes of our dedication.

Every time I think of the apostle Paul, I am reminded of a fictitious tale of a man walking into a lumbering camp and asking for a job. The foreman, noting that he was not a large person, said: "I'm not so sure you could handle it. It takes a real man to be a lumberjack."

"I am a man!" bristled the little fellow. "Just give me an ax and show me a tree; and if I don't get that tree on the ground in less than half the time it would take your best man in camp, I won't say any more about a job."

So they did that, and in the most marvelous and aggressive display of axmanship anyone ever saw, he had that tree on the ground in thirteen minutes. That was fifteen minutes faster than the best man in camp could have done.

The boss was amazed. "Where in the world did you learn to use an ax like that?" he asked.

"In the Sahara," the little fellow replied.

"The Sahara, man—that's a desert!" exclaimed the boss.

The man replied: "It is now."

Paul didn't cut down trees. Rather, he built up the kingdom of God. But Paul's life showed that same kind of aggressiveness. Let's read some statements of his found in Romans 1:14-16. Paul was writing to the people at Rome. He had not been there, but soon would be, and he was led of the Spirit to share his heart, his faith, and his love for Christ. He wrote:

> I am under obligation both to Greeks and to barbarians, both to the wise and to the foolish. Thus, for my part, I am eager to preach the gospel to you also who are in Rome. For I am not ashamed of the gospel, for it is the power of God for salvation to everyone who believes, to the Jew first and also to the Greek (NASB).

One never thinks of Christian dedication and sacrifice without thinking of Paul. This mighty mite, this jubilant little Jew, jogged along the roads of his day determined that all men everywhere should know Christ. He was Christ's first commando, attacking the strongholds of paganism with faith, sure that even though some battles would be lost the war would be won. Equipped with the whole armor of God, it never occurred to Paul that he ought to let up. "My greatest failure," he seemed to say, "would be to fail to go. Woe is me if I preach not the gospel."

Nothing could deter Paul. He climbed every mountain, overcame every obstacle, and scaled every wall that Satan put in his way. He wore scars like medals, proudly calling them "the marks of the Lord Jesus" (Gal. 6:17).

In Romans 1:14-16 are found the inspiration of Paul's life. You and I can take these statements and make them the mottoes of our dedication.

"I am debtor," said this great man. I have never known any great person who did not feel he owed his life to some cause. Paul's life seemed to say: "If Jesus Christ died that Calvary kind of death for me, no sacrifice is too great for me to make for him." Surely in his mind, Paul visited the cross daily and watched our Lord being crucified for all our sins.

He agreed with the poet who also made those mental pilgrimages to Golgotha and penned these lines: "It was His love for me that nailed Him to the tree, to die in agony for all my sins."[1] In his heart, Paul said: "If he loved me like that, I must return that love."

Another great truth will dawn upon the indebted soul:

> I will not only love him, but I will love all the people
> he loves. I will make it the first business of my life to
> see the world as my neighborhood. I am debtor
> both to the Greek, the barbarians, the wise and un-
> wise. I owe it to all people everywhere to tell them
> about Christ.

The next life-changing statement is this: "I am not ashamed of the gospel" of Christ. It has been said that silence is golden. But there are times when silence is yellow—a cowardly, sickly yellow. To remain silent about so great news as the gospel is treason of the soul. New Testament history backs up Paul's assertion of his eagerness to share Christ at any cost. Before Jewish and Roman authorities, while on trial for his life, chained to a soldier, in prison, in good times and bad, the testimony of Paul was consistently the same. "Look," he said, "one day I was walking down a road and something happened. That something was Someone. His name is Jesus, and he changed my life. Let me tell you what he can do for you."

A few years ago I was privileged to attend a Billy Graham crusade. A huge, new, professional stadium was the meeting place. On a Monday evening, our family was seated high up in the second tier. My son said, "Dad, do you have to make a decision to see what Astroturf looks like?"

I began to look around at that magnificent structure and wondered if we were using the facility to its best potential. For instance, it would be interesting, I thought, if the scoreboard clock could indicate how many minutes were left in the preacher's sermon. Or, perhaps we could get a running total of how many decisions were made. That's a good score to keep.

Then I saw the long rows of darkened rooms around the rim of the stadium: the press boxes. I knew if a football game was being played that night those rooms would be filled with men and equipment. Reporters would be interpreting to a viewing and listening audience the action on the field, explaining such strange terms as *crack-back block, flanker, tight end,* and *bomb*.

Wouldn't it be great, I pondered, if they were televising this event in the same way? One network might call it "ABC's Monday Night at the Crusade." In their press box would be three men: one, a somewhat sardonic professional reporter, and two ex-pulpit stars to lend color to the comments on the night's activity.

As the camera zoomed in on a seven thousand voice choir singing "Amazing Grace," Howie might say: "Don, you weren't much of a preacher in your day, but maybe you can tell us what 'amazing grace' means."

"Well, Howie, you need to know that it does not mean the blue-eyed blond down at the office. It speaks of a Heavenly Father who loves us so much he got into his world with us. He became a man. Because of that, we know that he knows what it's like down here, and we know what he's like up there—and that he loves us. He invites everyone to receive his love and his life. That's what 'amazing grace' means!"

Maybe during decision time, the camera could zoom in on someone kneeling with a counselor, accepting Christ. Several "instant replays" might be shown until everyone understands how to be saved.

The beginning of the service snapped my mind back to reality. But I've thought a lot of times since of how all of us are called to be "Good-Newscasters"—not to sit high in a stadium and interpret a crusade to a television audience but rather to go into our world, beyond the stained glass windows, and tell people that redemption has a meaning not related to trading stamps. We must tell them God in heaven loves them and wants to give them, through Christ, the best kind of life that never ends.

When we have established in our hearts that we are debtors, and that we are not ashamed of the gospel of Christ, then the next thing follows quite naturally: "I am ready!"

Paul understood full well the dangers involved in his sharing the gospel in Rome. Yet his courageous confidence in Christ prompted him to make a statement he later lived up to: "I am ready to preach the gospel to you that are at Rome also" (Rom. 1:15).

There is something in the grateful heart of a Christian which asserts: "Jesus, you are my Lord. I will go anywhere, do anything you want."

A man had just purchased an ancient automobile. He had made a good buy in the old Model T. As he drove the old Ford home, however, it stopped cold on a lonely stretch of highway. The stranded motorist didn't know how to uncover the engine, much less work on it.

At this moment, an apparently wealthy man in a gleaming new Lincoln pulled up and asked if he could help. "Anything you can do would be appreciated," said the owner of the ancient Ford. With skill and tenderness, the stranger uncovered the engine compartment and made an adjustment on the old carburetor. He set the spark lever on the steering column just right. Then, as he turned the crank, the old "Tin Lizzie" ran like the day it was made.

An amazed and grateful owner asserted: "Thank you, sir. You've helped me, and I don't even know your name."

"You're quite welcome," he replied. "My name is Henry Ford."

You see, Henry Ford knew how to make a Model T run because he made it. It is a matter of sanctified common sense to place our lives in the hands of God who can make them run smoothly because he made us.

A certain man's sister was so committed to the support

of missionary work that the man was certain she was called to be a missionary. He prayed daily that she would have the spiritual insight to recognize this calling. During one of those prayer times, our Lord convicted him that he was called to be a missionary. This world is filled with people who pray: "Lord, here am I; send my sister!"

Those who make a difference, however, are the committed who can say with Paul: "I am debtor. I am not ashamed of the gospel of Christ. I am ready! Here am I, send me."

Note

1. Norman J. Clayton, "For All My Sin," © 1943 Norman J. Clayton, assigned to Norman J. Clayton Publishing Co.

3

A Study in Elbows and Fingertips
Matthew 9:18-22
Mark 5:21-34
Luke 8:41-48

No matter how large the crowd, our Lord always knows the difference between elbows and fingertips. In many a gathering, scores of people rub elbows with God and never know it. Yet he is always sensitive to that one who reaches out to touch.

It shouldn't surprise us that the life of Christ is so amazing. Every time I read the gospel account of how he lived, something new comes up. Have you noticed how interruptions didn't seem to bother him? His whole ministry was one interruption after another—like this episode in Matthew 9. He was enjoying the company of some people when a group of Pharisees came and interrupted the party by asking, "Why are you associating with people like this?" While he was answering that question, some followers of John the Baptist interrupted and wanted to know why they fasted a lot but Jesus did not. Verse 18 states that while he was answering this, an important man in the city, named Jairus, rushed into the crowd and said, "Lord, my daughter is dying; you've got to come with me!"

Immediately Jesus followed him, and so did all the people at the meeting. As they were making their way down a narrow street, all crowded together and bumping into each other, Jesus suddenly stopped. Each must have bumped into the one in front of him like railroad cars. Then Jesus said a very strange thing. He asked, "Who touched me?" His disciples said, "Lord, this is a crowded place. Everyone is jostling against each other. What do you mean, 'Who touched me?' "

At this point a frightened, trembling lady stammered her story of healing. Herein lies one titanic truth. No matter how large the crowd, our Lord always knows the difference between elbows and fingertips. In many a gathering, scores of people rub elbows with God and never know it. Yet he is always sensitive to that one who reaches out to touch.

He clearly demonstrates here what he consistently illustrated in daily living. There are no unimportant people to God. On the way to heal the twelve-year-old daughter of the richest man in town, he paused to minister to a lady who had been an outcast for as long as the girl had lived. For twelve years she had been an outcast. She was not allowed to worship with God's people. She could not live in the community. She was not allowed to live with her husband and children. It was forbidden for her to touch another human. Now she had spent all her money. By every standard normally used to gauge human worth, she was bankrupt. She had lost acceptance, love, and wealth. Surely she said: "I am a nobody." But it was not so in the eyes of the Lord.

While many in the crowd, other than Jesus, agreed that she was no one, it is much closer to truth to note that she is everyone. Jesus came to this earth because he knows we are all as destitute in the eyes of God as this poor lady was in the eyes of her community. The Roman letter puts it like this: "For all have sinned, and come short of the glory of God" (Rom. 3:23). In another place, Holy Writ announces: "There is none righteous, no not one" (Rom. 3:10). For this reason a church must never see itself as an extension of country club exclusiveness. It is a sad day when a group called to be a family of Jesus Christ begins to see itself as some select society of splendid saints.

Like the woman, we must face our needs. We never begin to live until we frankly face the death that is in us. Every Christian knows he is a member of a society which could be rightly labeled "Sinners Unanimous."

The cure for such a malady is never found in just joining the crowd around Christ. It is not enough to merely push in with the people walking along beside him. You must reach out with fingertips of faith. He always knows the difference between elbows of unconcern and fingertips of faith.

He cares. He always responds to that reach, but note that it costs him to care. "But Jesus said, 'Someone did touch Me, for I was aware that power had gone out of Me' " (Luke 8:46, NASB). We get our word *dynamite* from the New Testament word *dunamis*. How gladly we share the good news of Christ, emphasizing that it is a gift. We cannot buy it, learn it, earn it, or seize it. We receive it by faith. Nothing is free. If you don't pay the price for something, someone else does. So it is with our salvation. Salvation is free to us because he paid the price. On the cross he paid the price for your sins and mine. What a thought to know that he cares for us, and he cares enough to pay a price like that!

Another amazing thing about his love is that at whatever point in life we discover there is nowhere else to go, we can come to him and he will accept us. This lady had tried everything else. For twelve years she had sought healing. Now all her money was gone; she couldn't afford to try another cure. When at last she came to Jesus, all she found was love and acceptance. How much tragedy, emptiness, and heartache is spared when we come to him soon. But soon or late, he loves you and wants to save you.

And when you come to him, you must come out of the crowd and announce yourself. This woman was healed when she touched his garment. Yet Jesus stopped and had her identify herself and testify to the others. It's true: You can accept Christ as your Lord and Savior right where you are. You can ask him to come into your life, forgive you of your sins, and be saved. But when you do that, he wants you to admit openly what you've done.

This woman had probably not heard a kind word in twelve years. Now she was hearing him say: "My daughter, your faith has made you well. Go in peace."

This may be the day you have decided to follow Jesus. You've tried a lot of things, and they haven't worked. Now you're coming to Jesus, not just to rub elbows with the people around him, but to reach out to Him. And you've received him as your Savior and Lord. You're saved! Now be sure to let it be known.

4

What Does It Take to Be Rid of Sin?
1 Corinthians 1:18-25

What sort of surgery of the soul is required to bring about a lasting cure of life's most deadly malady?

What does it take to be rid of sin? What sort of surgery of the soul is required to bring about a lasting cure of life's most deadly malady?

Very few people would argue against the presence of personal sin, even though they may have different names for it. Nations and families talk of peace and start wars. In the daylight there is talk of remorse for wrong, and nightfall finds the same sin coming back, bringing seven others with it. When our best efforts to master our own fates, captain our own souls, and work out our own destinies are damaged and destroyed by the contradictions in us, we identify with Paul's words of Romans 7: "Wretched man that I am! Who will set me free from the body of this death?" (v. 24, NASB).

There have been some classic answers to that question. There was the answer of the Jew. This is the claim that sins are taken away by an elaborate sacrificial system—the claim that we can find release through the rites of religious ritualism. The Jews, for the most part, had misunderstood the spiritual significance of the sacrificial system. It is to this fallacy the book of Hebrews asserts: "For it is impossible that the blood of bulls and goats should take away sins" (10:4, RSV).

Something keeps bringing up an answer like that—revised, of course, and brought up-to-date. Something tells us that surely in the externals of religion we can find some solution to the inner struggle of our souls. Somehow we feel if we do twenty-five spiritual pushups in the name of holiness, it can't hurt.

No greater mischief has ever befallen Christendom than that particular distortion which has imagined that divine grace could be materialized, fractionalized into units of varying value to facilitate transactions, and administered through the rites and requirements of an authoritarian, ecclesiastical organization. This malignant perversion has filled the records of Christian history with many a bloody page in its effort to establish and maintain an exclusive monopoly on saving grace. It has filled the heavens with demigods who have varying power to lobby in the throne room of the universe. It has endowed geographical locations and strange objects, such as dead men's bones, with marvelous religious significance. And it has made death a fearful inventory, even for the most faithful, in which one's debits and credits are audited to determine the extent of one's insolvency—replete with assignments to some purgatorial prison house to work off lingering indebtedness.

A time comes when the one who has trusted this sort of system begins to doubt. One of the greatest prophets said: "Wherewith shall I come before the Lord, and bow myself before the high God? shall I come before him with burnt offerings, with calves of a year old? Will the Lord be pleased with thousands of rams or with ten thousands of rivers of oil?" (Mic. 6:6-7a). The Word of God is bluntly emphatic in reply: "It is impossible that the blood of bulls and goats should take away sins" (RSV). All of our searching for the answer in some new religious thing to do is in vain. There is no answer there!

Others would tell us the answer to our sin is found not in something new to do, but in something new to feel or to think. "The Greeks seek after wisdom" (1 Cor. 1:22). Actually, the Greek mind has a double allegiance—to art and to philosophy. Hence the answer the Greeks gave to heal the hurt of humanity had two sides to it: aesthetic and intellectual. "We can," they would say, "overcome the radical illness of this world if we can only develop an awareness of beauty or if we can develop the logic of thought. The loveliness of nature can charm it away, or the wit of the philosopher can rationalize it away."

Ah, then we have some Greek in us too, don't we? There are a lot of folks who talk of communicating with God through nature. These feel it is more refreshing for the soul to head for the cabin than for church. While the beauty of nature is magnificent, it cannot do anything with our sin. No one has ever had sins forgiven in the name of the Grand Canyon.

Neither do games of mental gymnastics overcome our sin illness. Glossing over our guilt with intellectual coatings is like painting a termite-infested house. It may look good for a while, but the inner structure is being eaten away and will one day fall in ruins.

To all who say sin can be cured with something new to think or something new to feel, God says: "You must be born again" (John 3:7, NASB). New thoughts, new feelings, or new deeds are not what you need, but a new heart. Then that new creation of God in you will produce the proper thoughts, feelings, and deeds.

Righteousness is not a feeling of nostalgia on hearing a church bell ring. It is not a pensive mood incurred while standing on the shore of a crystal-clear lake. It is not a nebulous sense of wonder cast by the quiet glow of the setting sun. It is not a sophistication which allows God a place in the scheme of things. Salvation is the gift of the crucified and risen Christ given when one responds in faith to God's outreached grace. "For by grace you have been saved through faith; and that not of yourselves, it is the gift of God; not as a result of works, that no one should boast" (Eph. 2:8-9, NASB).

A third classic answer to the question of dealing with our sins is the answer of the Roman. This can be expressed in a single world, *moralism*. The Roman Empire, in its greatest hour, was known for law and order. The greatest of the Roman emperors were noted for their discipline and self-control. Yet sin corrupted that empire, just as it does even the strongest of men who set out to be good. In the first three chapters of his letter to the Romans, Paul vividly described what sin has done to every person on this earth. He makes a summary statement in Romans 3:23, "For all have sinned and fall short of the glory of God" (NASB). Our stoutest resolves and our most sincere declarations cannot overcome the force of sin in our lives.

The answer of moralism, like the answers of art, philosophy, and ritualism, all fail us. Over every human effort to overcome this sinful predicament there is written the judgment of frustration: "It is not possible. O wretched man that I am!"

But there is hope. Christ has done something. In Hebrews 9:26 we read it: "He has been manifested to put away sin by the sacrifice of Himself" (NASB). In our text Paul asserts: "But we preach Christ crucified, to Jews a stumbling block, and to Gentiles foolishness, but to those who are the called, both Jews and Greeks, Christ the power of God and the wisdom of God" (vv. 23-24, NASB).

So to deal successfully with our sins, you and I must go back to that strange, bare, skull-like hill just outside the north gate of Jerusalem. Rome chose that place for crucifixions because it was located next to the city garbage dump. We must look again at this pure, sincere Man— beaten of body and broken in heart, struggling under the weight of that cross until the loss of blood made him so weak he fell to the road with that hideous thing across his back. Yet face down, pinned prone in the dirt, he kept reaching back for that cross as though he wanted it, as though he had to have it, as though that thing were a part of him. When they got him to his feet he, with determination, trudged up that hill as though this thing had already been decided and had to be done. Hear again the

angry sounds of that mob, "Son of God, ha!" Then listen
to the dull thud of the blows of a heartless hammer as he
is nailed to that cross and see him, hanging there, paying
for your sins and mine.

You see, you and I must realize this death was occa-
sioned, not just by the actions of Pilate, Caiaphas, the
Jews, and the Roman soldiers, but by our sins.

A few years back a film was produced about the life of
Christ. Near the end of the picture, the crucifixion was
portrayed in all its gruesome pageantry. Then Jesus' body
was taken down from the cross and buried in Joseph's
tomb. The mob, along with the soldiers and the disciples, left the scene of his death. Three roughly-hewn
crosses stood silently against the turbulent heavens when
a lonely figure, with sin and desperation written across
his filthy countenance, stealthily made his way to the
center cross. Quivering with emotion from the experience, he flung himself at the foot of the cross. After a
long, long while, he hesitantly dared to look up where
Jesus had just hung and sobbed "He died for me. He died
for me!" Whether Barabbas ever realized it or not, Jesus
Christ actually did take his place that day at Calvary.
And, your name and mine is Barabbas!

What looked like an ignominious defeat was in reality
a glorious victory. If you call the cross history's blackest
crime, the trumpeting triumph of concentrated naked
demonism, you will be right. But God got his hands on
that demonic thing, and by a superb divine irony—like
David using Goliath's own sword to behead the giant—
he turned it into the devil's irrevocable defeat. Those
nails used to fasten him cruelly to that cross were common spikes. They could have been used to build a ship, a
bridge, or a home. But hate took those nails and said:
"These are my nails and with them I will destroy you."
Then Love received those nails and replied, "These are
my nails, and with them I will save you!"

A great Christian friend of mine, now a seminary professor, spoke of the day of his salvation: "I was walking," he said, "thinking about the cross and why it had to happen. I had always known Jesus Christ died on the cross, but in that moment I realized Jesus died on the cross for me." Is this your moment not just to believe that Jesus died on the cross, but to know Jesus died on the cross for *you*?

5

The Mystery of Who We Are
Genesis 1:27
Romans 7

"You preachers say God made us. Yet when we do things because of who we are, you tell us we are wrong and need to repent. If God made us like this, why are we wrong and what can we do about it anyhow?"

Preachers are often asked questions. Sometimes they are the old stock questions like: "Where did Cain get his wife?" The best answer is: "I'd tell you if I were Abel."

Every now and then, though, someone will ask a very good question. A student demanded: "You preachers say God made us. Yet when we do things because of who we are, you tell us we are wrong and need to repent. If God made us like this, why are we wrong and what could we do about it anyhow?" That, my friends, is a good question.

The answer begins in understanding that man is the only creature God didn't finish. You never see anyone pat a puppy on the head and say, "Well, little doggie, what are you going to be when you grow up?" He's going to be a dog! But little boys and girls can grow up to be a lot of different people because to us is given the dignity and the danger of decision.

As we grow older, we discover that our decisions have made us not one person, but several. We tend to be different people under different circumstances. Some lines illustrating this were penned by that popular, yet poorly paid poet, Anonymous:

> Within this earthly temple of me, there is a crowd.
> There is one of me that is humble, there is one of me
>   that is proud.
> There is one of me that loves his neighbor as himself.

There is one of me that loves naught but fame and
  self.
There is one of me that feels sorry when he sins.
There is one, that unrepentant, sits and grins.
From much undue anxiety I would be free
If only I could decide which one is me!

There are times when all of us feel like saying, "Will
the real me please stand up?" Does God have any word
to explain our strange condition? Are we forever to be
creatures of divided hearts? God not only describes the
condition that imprisons us, but also declares a way of
liberation. The Word tells us of Creation and Fall, of
civil war and futility, and of Christ and freedom.

The beginning words of the Bible speak to us of creation and fall. Genesis 1:27 tells us God created man in
his own image. God made man because he wanted fellowship with man. He made him different from the
other animals. Man's kinship with beasts is time's oldest
lie. God intended that man "have dominion," be in
charge of God's world.

If we could have visited Adam in the Garden of Eden
we probably would have been impressed with the place.

"Wow, Adam," we might ask, "Who owns this?"

"God does."

"Well, I'd like to look into this. Take me to the manager."

Adam would reply, "You're looking at him."

Adam and Eve, like you and I, were God's representa-
tives, made managers of God's things. We are man in
the middle—kin to God yet made of dust. We are both
dust and deity.

One thing is very apparent. God liked man. He likes
what he has created. He looked at man and said, "That
is good. That is very good!"

I hope you never forget how much God loves you. The
Bible is God saying, "I love you." While you and I must

face frankly our sinfulness, we must go on without hating ourselves. We must not hate what God loves so very much.

I remember when our church changed from the Broadman Hymnal to the Baptist Hymnal several years ago. In the old book there is a song that tells of Jesus dying on the cross "for such a worm as I" (Isaac Watts, "Alas, and Did My Savior Bleed," *The Broadman Hymnal*, © 1940, Broadman Press, p. 112). The new hymnal changed those words to say "a sinner such as I" (*Baptist Hymnal* 1975, p. 113). Now, when we sing that song I still get mixed up and often I am the only worm in the house! But I'm glad we changed it. Nowhere in all of God's Word do we hear him address us as worms. Sometimes people in the Bible call themselves worms, but God is always saying, "My son, my daughter, I love you." Even the severest of his judgments and the sharpest of his denunciations are aimed at getting us to put ourselves in a position to receive his love.

We are made in the image of God but marred by the ignominy of sin. You recall how the beautiful relationship between Adam, Eve, and God was marred because Satan entered the scene and convinced Adam and Eve they did not have to do all God said. "Assert your independence! Do your own thing!" he tempted. We all forfeit our fellowship with God when we do our thing and not his.

The little girl was visiting her grandparents in Washington, DC. As any good grandfather would do, he took her to the beautiful zoo in our nation's capitol. There the tragedy happened. She slipped away from her grandfather's side and crawled under the guardrail that kept people a safe distance from the lion's cage. Before anyone could do anything, the lion had pulled the little girl into the cage with him. In clear view of the helpless and hysterical grandfather that beast mauled the little girl to death. As he stood numbed and sobbing, the man re-

membered his granddaughter's last words. She had refused to hold his hand, saying: "I like to hold my own
hand, Grandfather."

All of the sin and heartbreak of this world has come
because man has refused to admit how dependent he is
upon God. "I like to hold my own hand, God," he declares, and he is mauled to spiritual death by Satan,
whom the Bible describes as our "adversary . . . who
prowls about like a roaring lion, seeking someone to de-
vour" (1 Pet. 5:8, NASB).

We often try to blame our sins on others. We say, "If
only I had different parents or friends," or "If circumstances were changed." But really we sin because we
choose to, because we say: "I like to hold my own hand,
God."

The pattern of blaming others for our mistakes is an
old one. Someone pictured Adam, Cain, and Abel walking past the Garden of Eden. Cain looked in and said,
"Say, Dad, that looks like a cool place to live. Why don't
we move in there?"

"Well, Son, we used to live there till your mother ate us
out of house and home!"

Being made in God's image and marred by sin brings
into our experience a severe state of unrest. Creation and
fall issues in us civil war and futility.

All of us know about Dr. Jekyll and Mr. Hyde, a story
of one man with two personalities. Dr. Henry Jekyll was
the outstanding citizen of his city. No one could think
wrong of him. He was, in the eyes of the people, above
reproach. One day he began to experiment with a mixture he concocted in his laboratory. All of his evil tenden-
cies forced their way to dominance in his life and he became Mr. Edward Hyde, the meanest man in town. He
could change from Dr. Jekyll to Mr. Hyde at his own
will. He was both good and bad.

Robert Louis Stevenson could well have conjured the
idea for his story from observing human nature, for there

is some Dr. Jekyll and Mr. Hyde in each of us. But I wonder if the author may have gotten his inspiration from reading the personal testimony penned by Paul in the seventh chapter of Romans. All of us can identify with that. We experience some difficulty in knowing what is right, but a much larger problem in consistently doing what is right.

The helpful county agent told the farmer he could furnish him with books that would help him be a better farmer, to which the man replied: "I already know how to farm better than I'm doing now."

There were days in the past when I thought I wanted to learn to play golf. I read books by Jack Nicklaus, Arnold Palmer, and Gary Player. The proper way to stroke a golf ball was firmly fixed in my mind. Then I went out to do it, and flubbed many an innocent golf ball into a watery grave! Bob Hope said he bought Arnold Palmer shoes, Arnold Palmer slacks, Arnold Palmer shirts, and Arnold Palmer clubs—then went out and played like Betsy Palmer!

A million times more serious is the sad fact that we can fix into our minds how good we could be and how well we could live, then we go out and fail to do it. In the story of Dr. Jekyll and Mr. Hyde there came a time when evil Edward Hyde could not change himself back to good Henry Jekyll. The bad had prevailed, and no matter how much he wanted to be good he could not accomplish it.

It is so with all of us. We are constantly losing the civil war that rages within us. By our own achievement we cannot do good in God's sight. When we realize this frustrating fact we join Paul in saying, "Wretched man that I am! Who shall set me free from the body of this death?" (Rom. 7:24, NASB).

Faith has an answer. It tells us of Christ and freedom. "I thank my God through Jesus Christ our Lord. He has set me free!"

Have you caught the full thrust of this good news from

God? Through Christ, the defeat and futility can be changed to victory and freedom. Our Lord is very anxious for you to know he loves you and what he can do for you.

Have you ever thought of how a baby discovers he is loved and gains a sense of importance? As he is held in his parents' loving arms, and those big people are speaking sweet things, something in that child says, "I don't know what they see in me. I can't do anything to help around here. I can't even keep my chin dry! But they must think I am somebody important. Just look at the way they look at me!"

This is much like the way we learn that God loves us. We look at that cross—that very cruel, humiliating, and painful death on the cross—and we say, "I don't know why he did that. He did not have to do that. If he did that for me, then he must think I'm somebody important."

And he does, my friend. He thinks you are important enough to die for.

Since Christ loves us so much, Paul had no trouble calling him "Lord." Freedom comes through commitment to "Jesus Christ our Lord" (Rom. 7:25, NASB), the Scriptures assert. You see, control is the secret of success or failure in living. When Adam and Eve decided to take over control of their lives they failed. So do we. The big test of faith is to ask: "Who is in control?" If Christ is in control, then you are free. As you daily give your life to his control, you keep on experiencing victory and freedom.

6

You Can Come Back

The Word of God is filled with true case histories of those who came back. The gospel of Jesus Christ is an invitation to begin again.

Think with me of some who came back. There was a conniving cheat named Jacob whose name was changed to Israel—"Son of God."

David, the great king, the mighty monarch, loved by God, adored by men, spiritual as well as governmental leader, shocked the kingdom with his dual sin of adultery and murder. He paid a huge price for those sins, wore their scars all his life, but he prayed, "Have mercy upon me, O God," and came all the way back to the Father's favor (see Ps. 51:1-4).

Then there is the case of the impetuous apostle who not only denied Christ but cursed at the sound of his name. Yet he came back to speak from those same lips, proclaiming the freedom in Christ for thousands of others.

Of course, the classic story exposing the heart, love, and invitation of God to come back is found in Luke 15. There was a younger son who said: "Dad, as far as I'm concerned, you're dead. Why don't we just act as though you had gone on. Give me my share of the inheritance now, and let me split." He stomped off to a foreign country and squandered both his money and himself.

But he came back. That's the point of the story. He came back. We are aware that this is more than just a nice story when we remember who is telling it. Jesus Christ, the Son of God, is telling us we can come back.

Let us zoom in for an instant replay on the key sentence, "And when he came to himself . . . " (Luke

15:17). These words mark the beginning of his return. Here realization dawns upon the sin-marked face of a once-proud young man that we must learn how to come back.

You can come back when you face yourself. "He came to himself" and said "I have sinned" (Luke 15:17,21). He faced up to himself as he really was.

A man entered a travel agency and told the clerk: "I want to travel—by boat, plane, train, bus—makes no difference. I just want to get away from myself for a while."

"Sir, I can't do that," replied the clerk. "I can sell you a ticket that will take you away from your work or your surroundings, but you cannot buy a ticket to take you away from yourself."

Since we can't get away from ourselves, we must eventually face up to ourselves. We can't divorce ourselves. We can't move away from ourselves.

When the Prodigal Son faced up to himself, he felt guilty. You and I spend a lot of time feeling guilty, don't we? Some sensitive persons feel guilty when they should not. Most of the time, however, we feel guilty because we are guilty. This young man felt guilty because he was guilty. If someone had said to him: "Don't feel guilty; don't be so hard on yourself," it would not have helped. He was guilty, and he had to face up to that fact just as you and I do at times. We face up to ourselves, look honestly at ourselves and say: "I have sinned." This is the first hard step in coming back.

The next step on the way back is to accept yourself. When we come to the excruciating pain of facing up— honestly—to ourselves, there are some things we could do. After you say: "I am a sinner!" What then? You must accept yourself for what you are.

We hear the word "neurotic" a lot. A neurotic is someone who suffers from the fact that he cannot accept himself and cannot endure himself.

Well, after you have faced up to yourself, what can

you do? There are several possibilities.

You can destroy yourself. You can say: "I'm just a no-good bum, no good to anyone, and I sure do feel sorry for me." So you find a way to destroy yourself. Through alcohol or drugs or self-pity, you rip yourself to pieces and bit-by-bit throw yourself away.

You could destroy others. Because you feel so little, you can find ways to make other people look little. This is why we gossip about others. Remember the motorcycle gang, "Hell's Angels"? Here is a classic example of people who could not accept themselves or their limitations, so they did things to shock other people, and they destroyed property because others had things they could never have.

Or, you could quit. You could just say: "Stop this world, man; I want to get off. I'm just playing it cool. Let the world be hanged while I recline."

Or, you could accept yourself. This means that, after you have admittedly faced up to yourself, you will say: "I recognize my limitations. I want to do better, but I have to start where I am."

In the play, *Green Pastures*, Noah says: "I ain't very much, but I'm all I got." That's terrible grammar but excellent philosophy!

In his sermon about the Prodigal, Peter Marshall pictured the Prodigal Son as the artistic one, taking after his deceased mother and having no inclination for farming and ranching at all. He persuaded his father to let him take his money so he could go to Paris to study art. But he soon learned his ambition overran his abilities. He either was not that talented or wasn't willing to pay the price to learn to paint. Soon he was caught up in the immoral life-style around him and quite quickly his money was gone.

At one time or another, each of us has to face up to our own limitations. So what if you're not a Rolls Royce—what if you're only a Ford! It is what you do with what you are that counts. The fact is, a well-handled Ford can go further than an ill-treated Rolls Royce. We have to start with what we've got.

Paul is a great example of accepting himself and external conditions. In Philippians 4:11-13, he asserted, "I have learned to be content in whatever circumstances I am. Whether it be plenty or poverty, sickness or health, that's fine, I have learned to be content" (author's words). The word *content* means "self-sufficient." In verse 13, he shared the secret for himself and for you and me: "I can do all things through Him who strengthens me" (NASB).

You can come back when you realize you are responsible for yourself.

There came an hour of awakening in which this young man not only faced up to himself and said: "I am a sinner," accepted himself as he really was, but also realized he was responsible for himself and for his actions. So he said: "I will arise and go to my father . . . " (Luke 15:18).

Taking responsibility is the main factor in coming back. Many face up to themselves, even accept themselves to a degree, but will not take responsibility for themselves. "It's his fault, her fault; it's their fault. If only we had a different President."

Every now and then I hear it. Probably, you hear it more than I. Someone will say: "The church has let me down. I have lived in this community for twenty years, and no one from the church has ever knocked on my door." Or, "I used to go to church there. When I dropped out, no one ever told me he missed me." When I hear sounds like that, I get guilt feelings. We are responsible, as his church, to care and to demonstrate that concern. Yet each time I hear someone speak like this, I want to ask: "Don't you care about yourself? We are responsible for you, that's true, but you are responsible for you, too."

The Bible has great promises God will gladly keep. Re-

member Jesus' saying: "Come unto me, all ye that labour
and are heavy laden, and I will give you rest" (Matt.
11:28). You see, it all depends on your willingness to take
the responsibility of coming to him.

If you've never given your heart to God, but you've
seen glimpses of what a great life it is to know Jesus, listen: "But as many as received him, to them gave he
power to become the sons of God" (John 1:12). If you
have come to Jesus, but you've drifted away from the
Father's heart and will and now you are homesick for his
righteousness, hear his promise: "If we confess our sins,
he is faithful and just to forgive us our sins, and to
cleanse us from all unrighteousness" (1 John 1:9).

But you must receive him before you can have life. You
must confess your sins and ask forgiveness before you can
have cleansing. You must respond to God for yourself.

It was a great day when the young man came home. It
set off a giant celebration. God's Word asserts that angels in heaven rejoice when you come to Christ (Luke
15:10).

How do you come back? How do you get this great
life? You don't get it by taking a trip, either physically or
mentally, nor by taking pills or drugs. You take a gift,
God's gift—forgiveness. It doesn't take a long time; you
can do it now. But it does take surrender. You just face
yourself, accept yourself, and realize you are responsible
for your own response to God. Then you say, with the
Prodigal Son, "I will arise and go to my father and will
say unto him, 'Father, I have sinned . . . And am no
more worthy to be called thy son; make me as one of thy
hired servants' " (Luke 15:18-19). Then, my friend, you
are back.

I hope you'll keep coming back. This world needs you.

7

Have You Found Yourself?
Matthew 16:25-26

I want to be free,
Free to be me:
To find the real self
Put on the shelf
By Satan's trickery.

Christ made me free,
Dying and living for me.
Now I can see
My way to liberty.
Identifying with him,
I find me.

There once was a boy who had great difficulty remembering where he had left things. So he wrote himself a note just before he went to sleep: "Your shoes are under the bed; your clothes are on the chair; your cap is hanging in the closet; your money, your knife, and your baseball cards are on the bureau; and you are in the bed." In the morning he found everything precisely as the note indicated, but when he looked in the bed, he was not there. So he could not find himself.

I am told a good businessman has an inventory indicating the location of every tool, every piece of equipment and material he owns. What a strange commentary on our lives—that modern man knows how to find things, but has a most difficult time finding himself.

A well-known German novelist, Hermann Hesse, asserted: "The true profession of a man is to find his way to himself. I have become a writer, but I have not become a human being." At the passing of a prominent man in one of the northern states, an editorial epitaph was composed, almost in jest, yet it tacks a terrible truth on the wall of our awareness: "Born a human being; Died a wholesale grocer." Now this is no dig aimed at grocers. It could be said of most all of us. Failing to find identity in ourselves, we seek it in possessions or position, neither of which are necessarily evil. Yet what a sad commentary on eternal souls made in his image. We have lost ourselves, and our struggle for identity is expressed in what we have or what we do—instead of who we are.

Dressing this great truth in common clothing, Jesus Christ asked: "For what shall it profit a man, if he shall gain the whole world, and lose his own soul?" (Mark 8:36). "Soul" means "life," "yourself," "you"! So he is declaring: "You, you who are always thinking in terms of profit and loss, let's take this thing all the way to the extreme. If you could own everything in, on, above, and under the earth, yet in the finding of that temporary stuff you lost yourself, you would have suffered a titanic loss."

Many times I have heard folk laugh at faith's simple words, "lost" and "found." Yet, in your heart, you know somewhere you have lost yourself. God's Word tells you how that happened and how to find yourself again.

The Word of God is an inventory of the soul, a guide, not for finding things, but for finding yourself. *You must first know where you lost yourself.*

An old country song entitled "Foolish Questions" spotlights some of the unthinking queries we often make in everyday conversation. For instance, one might state his intention to visit a friend in the hospital. In response comes a foolish question: "Is he sick?" One line in the song presents this interesting exchange: "I'm going to Ned's funeral." "Oh, is Ned dead?" To which you might as well reply, "No, he thought he'd have his funeral, then later on he'd die."

My mother had the annoying habit of asking one of those foolish questions. When I would come in childlike dependence declaring my loss of something of great value to me, she would always ask: "Well, son, where did you lose it?" If I had known where I lost it, it wouldn't have been lost!

Most of us do know we lost ourselves somewhere. There is a gnawing awareness that what we have become is so far short of what was originally possible. It is as though we were begun as original oil paintings done by a Master Artist, but somewhere along the way the

Master Artist has been replaced by an artless amateur who is slopping ugly brush strokes over the original. Now, whatever beautiful picture was begun is almost obliterated.

A new friend, Jane McCall, put it like this:

> It's raining outside. A tornado tore through Missouri and Kansas. News reports said the damage would run into millions of dollars. The governor declared a state of emergency.—It's raining inside. The storm hit and no one was around to estimate the damage. I'm too scared to look. How do you assess the wreckage of your life? How do I declare a state of emergency?

There is a state of emergency in the human soul. This is a foundation fact of our faith. The first three chapters of Romans are summed up in this statement: "For all have sinned, and come short of the glory of God" (Rom. 3:23). That much misunderstood and maligned little word, *sin*, describes the state of emergency in our souls. It means "perversion of purpose." We are not what God intended because of sin. It means "rupture of relationship." You were made for friendship with God. Sin separated you from him and an aching void, a hunger in the heart, has resulted.

Sin means "rebellion," and in this word is the answer to where you lost yourself. Genesis 1:27 declares: "So God created man in his own image, in the image of God created he him; male and female created he them." The story of Adam and Eve is your story and mine. We are made in God's image. That means we are created for God, to have fellowship with God, and to obey him. What a great life they had. They experienced joy and fulfillment, peace, and love. But something happened which fouled up that beautiful picture. Satan entered the scene and said, "Hey, you don't want to be images of

God, you want to be God. Don't let him tell you what to do. Do your own thing!"

As we carefully study the anatomy of the first spiritual murder we can see how Satan, the master liar and supreme con-artist of the ages, uses the same lines on you and me. If you have a view of Satan in red tights, pointed tail, complete with horns and pitchfork, forget it. A better picture would be the man of distinction or the playboy adviser. He comes convincingly disguised as one who will do you well, but is solely dedicated to doing you in. And he says, "Hey baby, you don't want to be God's image. You want to be God!"

All of us lost our identity when we tried to paint our own self-portrait over the image of God. The identity crisis was born in the womb of man's first sin. You see, when the Bible asserts you and I have sinned and have rebelled against God, it doesn't mean we accidentally lost ourselves. It is declaring we were tricked into throwing ourselves away.

The first step in being found, repentance, means you recognize this and you say: "Lord, I am sorry I rebelled against your will. I confess my sin of letting you down and fouling me up."

You must know not only where you lost yourself, but also where to find yourself. That image, that identity, that self lost in sin, is found in Christ. The broken and lost image of God shines again in Christ. Colossians 1:15 presents him as the image of the invisible God.

He is the true pattern for human living. He is the perfect picture of what God had in mind when he said: "Now I'll make me a man." We can find our identity in Christ. A college student said: "I studied Jesus Christ, not just to learn who he was, but to know who I am." Bishop Stephen Neill has been quoted: "Before the lost image of God in man can be restored, that true human reality into which man is to be transformed must visibly be set before his eyes. This it was that was accomplished in the life and death of Jesus of Nazareth."

The true pattern for our living is in Christ. In our proud arrogance we say: "I am all I need. I can do it, and I can do it my way." How many wrecks on that proud, foolish road could be averted if we would identify with him who spent much of his time praying, seeking his Father's will and strength. As a preacher it is very easy for me to get involved in speaking concepts, in merely talking love. Yet I look at Christ and realize he didn't just preach about leprosy, he touched a leper. He did not merely lecture on hunger, he fed hungry people.

But he is much more than just a pattern to show us what we should be. He is a Savior to empower us to be the selves we could never be without him. When you invite Jesus Christ to come into your life, he begins a process whereby you become a new person.

God sent Jesus not just to be a great ideal, but to die and come alive again in those who know him. How comforting it is when we are sick to be in the presence of a doctor. Yet if we didn't understand the purpose of the doctor, we'd be offended by his presence. A healthy doctor, towering over our weak, sick bodies, would only emphasize our sickness more if we didn't know he was there to help us be well like himself. Christ didn't come to be a perfect person just to point out our imperfections, but to make us like himself. That's why the Bible doesn't tell us to try to be like Christ—rather it says: "Put . . . on the Lord Jesus Christ" (Rom. 13:14).

Paul called himself "a man in Christ." A Christian has an identity. He has found himself in Christ. He says: "I know my *past*—where I came from. I know where I went wrong. I tried to play God instead of being satisfied to be a real person. I know my *future*—my destiny is in Christ. I know the *present*—I can face myself now, my problems, my hang-ups, my assets, and my faults. I have turned myself over to God!"

I find a great delightful paradox. Becoming more and

more by God's power like Jesus Christ, I don't become less and less Frank Pollard. Only as I become like Christ can I become what Frank Pollard was meant to be.

Bob Slocum, a physicist with Texas Instruments who develops space instruments for NASA said:

> I became convinced that Jesus Christ is the God behind the physical universe. The important question then became not whether I thought God was real, but whether God thought I was real. The idea took hold that in Christ, God does love me and takes me seriously. And I began the experience of placing my life in His hands and setting out to discover what it means to live for Him.

You can find yourself in Christ. There are three "you's." The "you" you think you are; the "you" others think you are; and the beautiful "you" God knows you are and through Christ can cause you to be! You can find yourself in Christ.

8

Anatomy of a Spiritual Murder
Genesis 3

There is a growing awareness among discerning folk today that they've been had. They have been tricked. They have followed all the enticing invitations posted along the way. "This Way To Success"—and they ran down that road until their sides were aching and they finally realized the road became steeper and more demanding, and the definition of success kept changing. "This Way To Happiness"—and they dashed down that road until they began to notice all the unhappy people coming back.

A young preacher observed that hundreds of cars drove by his church daily, apparently without noticing it. So he called a staff meeting to discuss what might be done. They decided to put up a sign right by the busy street. The sign read: "IF YOU'RE TIRED OF SIN, COME ON IN." A few days later someone had written on the bottom: "IF NOT, CALL 899-3334."

Some people are not tired of sin. Yet there is a growing awareness among discerning folk today that they have "been had." They've been tricked. They have followed all the enticing invitations posted along the way. "This Way To Success"—and they ran down that road until their sides were aching, and they finally realized the road became steeper and more demanding, and the definition of success kept changing. "This Way To Happiness" said another indicator, and they dashed down that road until they began to notice all the unhappy people coming back.

The fleeing Nazis in World War II were being chased out of France. As they retreated, they changed all the road signs, a trick that confused the Allied Armies and sent them in many a wrong direction until it was realized those signs could not be trusted.

A lot of people are becoming aware that some enemy has changed the signs. He has posted his false directions in many attractive and creative ways, using the best and cleverest minds and media. "Here is life!"—and he sends you toward death. "Here is happiness!" he invites, and you soon learn he has changed the street sign. That was not "Happiness Boulevard" at all. It was "Misery Avenue." His motto is: "Promise them anything, but give them hell."

In the third chapter of Genesis we see him making his first pitch: stealing life, happiness, and fellowship with God away from Adam and Eve. It may or may not be surprising to discover he hasn't changed his line one bit. Why should he? It is still working. The things he said to Eve, he is still saying to you and me. As we look at this Anatomy of a Spiritual Murder, we are not dissecting ancient history. Rather, we are studying the battle strategy of our greatest enemy—a strategy he will probably employ on you and me before the day is over.

Satan came as a serpent, the Scripture states. You'll notice this was before the serpent was a snake. It was a beautiful creature, shining, flying, and talking. My, how this must have impressed Eve! None of the other creatures talked. "Why, this is a miracle," she must have said. "I must listen to this beautiful creature!" Satan was appearing as he always does—as an angel of light with false credentials. He presents his lies today in much more impressive and subtle ways than most truth is presented. Wise people quickly learn that right is right no matter how poorly stated, and wrong is wrong even if it is impressively presented.

No small number of biblical observers have noted that Satan tempted Eve, and she in turn tempted Adam. Maybe Satan did approach her first because he thought she was most vulnerable, but verse 6 seems to indicate that her husband was right there with her all the time.

The Bible implies that Eve was deceived by Satan, but Adam apparently was not. There is no indication that Adam doubted God's Word one bit. Adam's sin seems to have been that he preferred his woman to his God.

When he came to a choice he did what the woman wanted rather than what God wanted. Many a man and woman have done this.

But all of that is not the big reason this Scripture is given to us. God has recorded for you and me the method of operation of our craftiest and deadliest enemy. He always comes cleverly disguised as one who will do you good, but in reality is committed to doing you in.

Satan begins by questioning the goodness of God. "Really, Eve," he said, "Is God doing everything for you he should? Are you allowed to have all the good things in this place?" He did not mention all the good things God had given them to enjoy (which he was going to trick them into losing). He just pointed out the one thing they were not to touch.

Tell me, does someone or something ever suggest that God is trying to keep something from you; that there is more to life than you'll really be able to enjoy if you obey God?

When Jesus was tempted out in the wilderness, Satan suggested the same thing to him. "If you really are the Son of God, turn these stones into bread. You've been out here living on juices and water for forty days. If you are the Son of God, he ought to feed you. He is withholding something from you. God is unkind. He is not good" (author's words). Believe me, my friend, it is no accident that this particular thought has popped into our minds.

Now after Satan subtly suggests that God is not good, he turns to say that God is too good. Eve told him that God said they were not to eat of the tree in the midst of the Garden or they would die. "You won't die," hissed Satan. "Why, do you think a loving God would let a thing like that happen to you?"

That isn't very consistent, is it? In fact, it is kind of dumb. But we want so much to believe Satan, so we say: "That's right. God is not good. He is trying to keep some-

thing from me." Then we reason: "But I know if I disobey him, He won't punish me because he is good, and a
loving God wouldn't do that."

Satan tried this on Jesus in the wilderness, too. He
took him to the roof of the highest building in the city
and said, in effect: "The way to really get people to follow you is to do some giant spiritual trick. Give them a
religious magic show, and they'll flock after you. Just
jump off this building if you really are the Son of God;
even if you disobey him, he won't let you die."

The third temptation is the real kicker. Here Satan
slanders the motive of God. "For God doth know that in
the day you eat thereof, then your eyes shall be opened,
and ye shall be as gods, knowing good and evil" (Gen. 3:5).

He is saying God is selfish and jealous and is trying to
keep you out of a kingdom that is rightfully yours. Again,
this is what Satan told Jesus in the wilderness. He
showed Jesus all the real estate and people of the world
and said: "You ought to own all this; because of your
loyalty to God, he is keeping you poverty stricken" (author's words).

Has Satan ever told you that you are above all this
need for a Heavenly Father? That God is an opiate for
the masses who are less enlightened than you? "Go
ahead man, kick off those phony shackles. You've got
what it takes! God is trying to keep you from knowing
that. He's trying to keep you from discovering that you
are really a god yourself."

That's what he was saying to Eve and has said to
everyone who has walked this earth. Many people believe it. They breathe God's air; live by his grace; shake
their little fist in the face of God; and in their most resonant voice, which must sound terribly tiny, empty, and
squeaky to him, they say, "I'll do it my way!"

If such people were to gather to worship and state
their creed, it would go like this: "I believe in almighty
man; reducer of the atom, conqueror of space, and in the

progress which is his offspring and our only hope."

After this congregational statement of belief might come the singing of a devilish doxology: "Praise men from whom all blessings flow. Praise kingdom builders here below. Praise all who live by brotherhood. Praise goodness and make evil good."

The reason Satan's temptations sound good to us is because there is an element of truth in each one. Satan knows we can handle outright lies, but a half lie is most dangerous. Alfred Tennyson once said: "A lie that is all a lie may be met and fought outright; but a lie that is partly truth is a harder matter to fight."

Satan asked: "Yea, hath God said, Ye shall not eat of every tree of the garden?" (Gen. 3:1). Well, that was true. That was what God said, but it was phrased in such a way, with such a veiled suggestion, that it was a lie.

He comes today, at the proper moment, saying:

> Did God really say you are not to love anything or anyone more than me? Did he actually say you are to remember the sabbath day to keep it holy? Every one of them? Thou shalt not steal. . . . In today's society? Honor *your* father and mother? Thou shalt not commit adultery. . . . Really? Have you read *Cosmopolitan?*

He told them, "You shall not surely die." That was a half lie. There was an element of truth in the statement. They did not die a physical death immediately, but they did die a disastrous spiritual death. Their sin did what sin always does. It separated them from God and his blessings.

Again Satan said: "For God knows that in the day you eat from it [the tree] your eyes will be opened, and you will be like God, knowing good and evil" (Gen. 3:5, NASB). And when they yielded, they did know. But it was certainly not what they were led to believe. When they ate that fruit, their eyes were opened. So what the devil said was true, yet it was false. While knowledge came to them of good, it was of a good that became lost. They learned about evil all right, but it was evil by experience without the power to resist it. Their eyes were opened to know good without the power to do it and to know evil without the power to shun it.

You and I know what they experienced, don't we? Satan tempts, "Go ahead, try it. You'll like it. Don't think you're going to die; it won't hurt you." He told a half truth. We tried it and did like it—at first. Then we began to see. To see that we had given up good; to see that what we were doing was evil; but we were caught up in it, unable to get away from it, and it was taking us down a road altogether different than we imagined.

When we sin, something always happens. Immediately after their sin, Adam and Eve were afraid of God. They had never been afraid of him before. Had he changed? No. They had changed. Are you afraid of God? Are you afraid of anything?

They felt shame. "They knew that they were naked" (Gen. 3:7, NASB), the Scripture asserts. They became aware of their sins.

They experienced utter, helpless dejection. They tried to hide. They could not. You can't hide from God, but they tried because they didn't know what else to do. When God found them in their utter dejection, they began to blame others for their mistake. Adam blamed Eve; Eve blamed the serpent. Tell me, when you get caught, do you try to place the blame on someone else? "If he or she were different, I would be different."

That's the way sin works in our lives. It leaves us helpless and dejected, afraid and ashamed. Satan tells us we will "be as God. You will be somebody." But, when his work is completed, he leaves us much less than the creatures we were before.

Now what can be done? When in some manner God confronts us with our sin, what can we do? We can look at our sin in three ways. We may say: "It is impossible to forgive me my sins." I have heard people almost say, "No God in his right mind would forgive me my sins."

We may jump all the way across the road of truth and fall in the opposite ditch. "Of course God forgives sins. That's what he's for." Both of these are wrong. The former sees forgiveness as too hard, almost impossible. The latter views it as too easy, almost nonchalant.

The right way to handle sin is to face up to it in all its ugliness. Just as Satan comes looking so good, intelligent, and sharp—when he has done his work you see him as the dirty snake he is. You come to see that he has injected into your moral bloodstream the world's deadliest venom. What at first looked so proper and pleasing is now seen to be poison, and it will cause your eternal death.

Genesis 3:15 is the first prophesy concerning how God in his love did something about our sins. The death of Christ on that cross in Jerusalem was a costly and unspeakable gift. It took that to pay for your sins and mine.

James 1:14-15 give us the vivid description of how sin works in us to bring death: "But every man is tempted, when he is drawn away of his own lust, and enticed. Then when lust hath conceived, it bringeth forth sin: and sin, when it is finished, bringeth forth death."

John 3:16 describes how Christ has come to turn that death into life. "For God so loved the world, that He gave His only begotten Son, that whoever believes in Him should not perish, but have eternal life" (NASB).

Romans 6:23 puts both of these facts together for us. "For the wages of sin is death, but the free gift of God is eternal life in Christ Jesus our Lord" (NASB).

You don't have to run and hide in the noise and activity of the world. The God of grace is following you with a pardon in his hand.

9
Anatomy of a Backsliding
Mark 14

You always slide downhill. No one ever slid uphill. Backsliding, for a Christian, means regressing to a lower level of spiritual living.

Yogi Berra once said: "Before I start talking I want to say something." Yogi does have a strange way with words. Concerning the lack of turnout for a baseball game, he said: "If they don't want to come, you can't stop them."

Now all word-witchery does not center in Yogi Berra. A friend of mine, a well-known Baptist minister, wrote a book entitled, *Don't Miss It If You Can*. Even when you're not trying to cause it, words sometime arrange themselves in strange ways, especially in church bulletins. A pastor I know was leaving town on Monday afternoon. He instructed his secretary to insert a sermon title for the Sunday night service and told her just to put something in the bulletin to indicate he was going to be there Sunday morning. She followed his instructions. In the morning service schedule was a line saying, "The Pastor Speaks." The evening order of service contained the title he had given her: "What The Fool Said."

I once preached from this fourteenth chapter of Mark and entitled the sermon: "The Anatomy of a Backsliding." Somehow, the usual quotation marks were left off the bulletin. Usually the sermon title is stated in quotes and then on the same line is the word *Pastor*, indicating who is going to talk about the subject mentioned. Well, on that Sunday they left the quotes off and it read: "The Anatomy of a Backsliding Pastor."

The truth is, it could be my backsliding, or yours.

To backslide means to slide back. I'm sure you're glad to get that information. You always slide downhill. No one ever slid uphill. Backsliding for a Christian means to regress to a lower level of spiritual living.

In Mark 14 we are told of the backsliding of one of our Lord's best men. Simon Peter had been the first person to say: "Thou art the Christ" (Mark 8:29, NASB). Not only was he one of twelve men chosen to serve Christ as an apostle, he was one of the very select group of three apostles who were extremely close to Christ. Yet he slid away from his commitment to our Lord.

On Thursday night, about eight o'clock, he said to Christ, "I will lay down my life for You" (John 13:37, NASB). Around nine o'clock, he drew his sword to fight for Christ. About ten o'clock, he stood around a fire and denied even knowing Christ. What happened?

Whence comes spiritual cowardice like this? What causes a man to walk three years in one direction and then in one night surrender it all? How could the first person ever to confess: "Thou art the Christ" be the same man who cursed and said: "I don't know him"?

The Scripture traces the downward slope of Peter's regression. We do well to take note.

It began immediately after his great confession of faith in Christ. At this point our Lord began to speak of his purpose. He talked of a cross and his own death. This was shocking talk to Simon Peter. "No, Lord, you can't die on a cross. We won't have it!" The response of our Lord to this was stern: "Get behind Me, Satan," (Mark 8:33, NASB), he said to Simon—in effect "You're tempting me just like Satan."

This incident apparently arrested the spiritual growth of Simon Peter. While he stayed committed to Christ, he refused to believe our Lord knew best.

Then on that crucial Thursday night, Christ said: "You will all fall away from me tonight and be scattered like sheep." "You don't know what you're talking about," replied Simon Peter. "All these other guys may run, but not me!" Sadly Christ informed him: "Before the rooster announces Friday's dawn the second time you will have denied me three times." "Not so," retorted Peter. "Even if I have to die with you, I will never disown you."

At this point they entered Gethsemane. Peter, James, and John were asked especially to pray for our Lord, but they were tired and they slept. When Jesus came the third time to wake them up, he said: "Let's go; my enemies are here for me."

Suddenly Simon Peter was wide awake. He hadn't felt like praying, but he was ready to fight! A bystander named Malchus found himself confronted by a frenzied man who was surely the worst swordsman in southern Palestine. Peter tried to cut his head off, but all he got was an ear. For this military uprising, Simon Peter was once again rebuked by our Lord. You can almost hear him pout in confusion: "He doesn't like anything I do. No matter how hard I try, it always turns out wrong."

When they took Christ, Simon followed at a very safe distance. Waiting at the palace courtyard, he was chilled. So he gathered around a fire with others waiting there. Twice a young girl said: "You're one of his followers, aren't you?" And twice he denied knowing Christ. Then the others joined in: "Yes, you are! You're a Jesus man."

"No, no, I'm not. I don't know who you're talking about," and he dragged out some old fisherman language to underscore his denial. In the moments that followed, he saw Christ; he heard the rooster crow; and he broke down and wept.

As we trace the trail of his falling we can learn much, for almost all slidings are similar. It all begins when we say: "Lord, I know more than you do." The cross for Christ, and for you and me, means the will of God. While Peter would not accept this will of God for Jesus' life, too many of us will not accept the will of God for our own lives. The slipping begins when we say, "My way, Lord, not yours."

Boastfulness and conceit is the next step, causing us to slip. Many Christians may say: "Even though others stumble and fall, my Christian maturity is such that I will never forsake you." When you trot out an attitude like that, watch out! The Bible correctly asserts: "Pride goeth before destruction, and a haughty spirit before a fall" (Prov. 16:18) and is full of case histories to prove it.

Overconfidence always causes us to let up in our prayer life. "After all," we might say, "why would a spiritual giant like me need to do all that praying? I've got to get my beauty sleep."

Failure to pray can cause us to do the wrong thing, because we haven't sought God's will. Peter didn't pray, so when the time of action came, he made a mistake.

Even as zeal without knowledge produces confusion, so there comes a time of slackening of zeal. Like Peter, the backsliding Christian follows from afar. In fact, he gets progressively further away. He begins to stay at home from prayer service. Then he attends only one service on Sundays. Finally, he convinces himself how badly he needs the whole day to relax.

When you follow Jesus only when it is convenient—from afar—you get cold. Usually a backsliding Christian will try to warm himself at the world's fires. And in that crowd, someone may say: "I thought you were a Christian. What are you doing here?" And when that happens, anything short of repentance is denial.

The story doesn't end here. Simon Peter repented, came all the way back, and became the greatest preacher of his day. You can do the same. You can come back—all the way back. I pray you will.

10

Guard What Gets into Your Head
John 8:3-11
Romans 12:1-2

All your sin begins in your mind. If you are hopelessly controlled by some sinful weakness, it is because you have lost your head. If you are going to win over sin, you must get your head back.

The Scriptural episode of Christ's dealings with the woman caught in the act of adultery spotlights the character of God—a character which is consistent with the Bible's portrayal of sin. How wrong it is to think that God regards sin lightly, forgiving us when we casually ask him to, because, after all, it's his business to forgive sin. Not so! He takes sin seriously and never dismisses it lightly. He hates sin because he loves people, and sin never helps people. It always hurts them.

God is not some cosmic tyrant who is mad at you because you broke his rules. If the life of Christ tells us anything about God, it is that he is totally unconcerned with needless rules, especially religious ones. He is a loving God who knows that the force which causes you to break moral rules is the cause of all the agony, disease, and death in this world. Because he loves you, he doesn't take lightly that which makes your life miserable, apprehensive, and temporary—when he intends it to be abundant, joyous, and eternal.

When this woman was forcefully ushered into the presence of Christ, she probably had the same attitude you and I have when we are caught red-handed. She may have, at first, protested that there was nothing really wrong with what she had done. After all, why should society decide what two consenting adults should do? It is the normal pattern of human pride to react, when confronted with our sins, with more anger than sorrow. I'm sure she was frightened. It's true the chances were remote that they'd really stone her to death, but they were talking about it. Then shame crept in, tardy as usual. Shame always seems to arrive late, but it stays longer.

What a strange mixture of question marks and exclamation points must have paraded through her mind as she heard him turn the judgment from the accused to the accusers. By simply scratching a few words in the dirt, he stripped them of their judicial robes of righteousness. Here we learn a good deal about the mind of our Lord. The grace of his love would not condemn her, nor would the salt of his righteousness condone her sin. Her sinful act could be forgiven, but it must also be forsaken. "Neither do I condemn you; go your way; from now on sin no more" (John 8:11, NASB).

Have you wondered if she ever sinned again? Maybe you have wondered, for personal reasons. Does it bother you to read Hebrews 12:1-2, which tells us as Christians to "lay aside every encumbrance, and the sin which so easily entangles us" (NASB), so we can run a better race in his will? Perhaps it does.

Is there a Christian anywhere who does not regretfully remember what it is to sin against God, to be truly sorry, and hear him say: "Neither do I condemn you; go your way; from now on sin no more." But the sinful deed was repeated. Haven't all of us, more times than we want to remember, had to go before the throne of God praying: "O Lord, I've done it again!" Soon we honestly ask: "Can nothing be done? Must one be forever at the mercy of this ruinous repetition of wrong, repentance, and return to wrong?"

There is good news! The Word of God does have something to say. Winston Churchill is reported to have advised:

> Get one idea—one, not two, and give it a whack!
> Talk on a little while, then give your idea another
> whack! Talk some more and give it still another

whack! Proceed until you come to the finale, and
give it a terrific whack![1]

Here is the first biblical truth we must grasp if we will
overcome this terrific force within us. If you don't get
this, all other truths about sins working in you will not
help. If you would allow God to liberate you from sin's
power you must, for the rest of your life, keep giving this
truth a terrific whack! Here it is: All your sin begins in
your mind. If you are hopelessly controlled by some sinful weakness, it is because you have lost your head. If you
are going to win over sin, you must get your mind back.

You know how sin works, don't you? There are at
least two Scriptures which spell it out with unmistakable
clarity. Listen: Psalm 1:1, "How blessed is the man who
does not walk in the counsel of the wicked,/Nor stand in
the path of sinners,/Nor sit in the seat of scoffers!"
(NASB). James 1:14-15, "But each one is tempted, when
he is carried away and enticed by his own lust. Then
when lust has conceived, it gives birth to sin; and when
sin is accomplished, it brings forth death" (NASB).

The Psalmist significantly says that before a person
walks in the way of sinners and sits down to fellowship
with those who scorn God's ways, he first begins to think
like sinners and scorners. He listens to the counsel of the
ungodly. By divine inspiration and from sad observa-
tion, James notes the cycle of sin. All of our temptations
come from within us. Like an unsuspecting fish looking
at and desiring the luscious worm dangling before him,
you can allow the mind to desire, wish for and dream,
until even though you know the hook is there, you bite
away. It all begins in the mind.

Remember those strange words of our Lord in the Sermon on the Mount? "You have heard that the ancients
were told, 'You shall not murder.' . . . But I say to you
that every one who is angry with his brother shall be
guilty before the court. . . . You have heard that it was

said, 'You shall not commit adultery'; but I say to you, that every one who looks on a woman to lust for her has committed adultery with her already in his heart" (Matt. 5:21,22,27,28, NASB).

Do you see it? You are just as responsible before God for what you think as for what you do. Long before William James said "We become what we think," the Word of God asserted "For as he thinketh in his heart, so is he" (Prov. 23:7).

If you are caught up in some sin cycle, it happened because you lost control of your head. Now it has nothing to do with intelligence, supposed sophistication, or position in life.

Take the sin of adultery. The "up and out" of the country clubs call it a "meaningful affair." On a lower social strata, one is said to be "running around on his old lady or her old man." It is the same sin. It began in the same way. It is the result of what Zig Ziglar calls "stinkin' thinkin'."

How about stealing? The corporate whiz, using elaborate accounting procedures, swindles the stockholders. The construction worker walks off the job with the boss's tools. Same sin. Same source. A long list of sins could be compiled, but the source for every wrong act is the same. You fail because you don't watch what gets into your mind. A constant checkup from the neck up is needed. Your sin always comes the same way. Someone took over your head.

It probably wasn't a fast, one-attack assault. It may have happened very slowly over a period of years. Some of us can remember when what we saw in magazines, movies, and media was quite different from what it is now. It has been like living in a deteriorating neighborhood. The neglect comes gradually. Beautiful houses are simply left unpainted. Trash blows in and is picked up less regularly. More and more, ragweeds and dandelions replace roses and deep, lush lawns. The overall disrepair and trashiness is unconsciously and quietly encouraged by unconcerned people living side by side. They hardly notice what has happened. But let people who once proudly owned a home in that section return after ten years or so. They look with shocked disbelief at the appalling mess. Our national garden is becoming a garbage dump so gradually that most do not notice. The young think this is the way it has always been. And, irony of ironies, it is all defended in the name of enlightenment. If history tells us anything, it assures us we are not being enlightened, we are being entombed. One of the things the Bible means in advising that you keep yourself "unspotted from the world" (Jas. 1:27) is that you and I must stop letting the world dump its garbage on us. We must get our minds back!

The first step is to determine to change your mind about sin. All too many think the word *repent* is a stained-glass word. Don't be afraid of it. It simply means to change your mind. To repent of sin means to change your mind about sin. It means you begin to win over the force of sin in you when you say: "Lord, Christ, I'm sorry I sinned. On the promise of your Word and through your grace, I accept your cleansing." But it also teaches that you will guard your mind against sinful thoughts. You will stand guard over what gets into your head!

Listen to 1 Timothy 4:16, "Pay close attention to yourself and to your teaching; persevere in these things . . . " (NASB). Or, as it reads in another translation, "Keep a close watch on all you do and think . . . " (TLB). In 2 Timothy 2:22, this advice is found: "Run from anything that gives you . . . evil thoughts . . . stay close to anything that makes you want to do right" (TLB).

Standing guard over what gets into your head is both positive and negative. You will say to some thoughts, "You can't come in."

For instance, many radio stations in many cities have

realized how people are conditioned by repetition. Hearing an idea over and over has a great effect on people. Therefore, out of a sense of concerned responsibility, the management of these stations has decided not to play the so-called "sex-rock" and "drug-rock" records. Unfortunately, the management of some local stations has not yet made such a decision, so it is up to you to keep alert and not let a radio dump just any garbage in your mind.

Some adults are greatly influenced toward sexual looseness by reading modern novels and articles in periodicals and certain newspapers. You need to choose what you read carefully. Some may have to change friends. Each of you will have to determine for yourself what God's Word is pointing you to do when it demands that you "Run from anything that gives you . . . evil thoughts."

Guarding your thoughts must also be positive. You can't just say: "I'm not going to think about that," because that makes you think of it. You must find something positive to claim your mind's attention. Hear God's Word in Philippians 4:8:

> Finally, brethren, whatever is true, whatever is honorable, whatever is right, whatever is pure, whatever is lovely, whatever is of good repute, if there is any excellence and if anything worthy of praise, let your mind dwell on these things (NASB).

Here are some things you can do: Discipline yourself to read God's Word daily. It is powerful, positive food for your mind. Memorize some of God's Word. At any time you are tempted, you can call to mind the words of the Bible. Develop an interest in some wholesome activity. Develop a good, positive attitude, with an optimistic attitude toward life.

Here is another thing the Bible teaches: Don't dwell on the past. A recent survey indicated that when people awake in the mornings, 60 percent of them immediately think about the problems and failures of yesterday, 20 percent think about today, and 20 percent think of tomorrow. How better would our attitudes be if that 60 percent of mental energy wasted on things that cannot change could be aimed at the present? In Philippians 3:13-14, Paul said, "This one thing I do, forgetting those things which are behind, and reaching forth unto those things which are before, I press toward the mark for the prize of the high calling of God in Christ Jesus."

Now hear the highest truth of all: Romans 12:2. God's Word notes two kinds of people: those who are pressed into a mold by the world around them, and those who are transformed by the power of God within them. Listen: "And be not conformed to this world: but be ye transformed by the renewing of your mind. . . ." When you receive Christ, he comes into your life. And as you daily develop habits that open your mind to the power and fullness of God, you are constantly being transformed.

11

Handling the Hypocrite in Us
Matthew 6:1-5

When the Son of God walked this earth, he waged open war on hypocrisy. You and I watch some people who are such terrible actors play parts, and their hypocrisy is hilarious to us. But phonies were never funny to him. Although our Lord told his most humorous stories in exposing the hypocrites, he hated with holy vehemence the sin of hypocrisy.

If you have never acted as though you were something you are not, if you have never wanted others to think you are better or worse, stronger or weaker than you really are, this message is not for you.

One thing is for sure. When the Son of God walked this earth, he waged open war on hypocrisy. You and I watch some people who are such terrible actors play parts, and their hypocrisy is hilarious to us. But phonies were never funny to him. Although our Lord told his most humorous stories in exposing the hypocrites, he hated with holy vehemence the sin of hypocrisy.

What is a hypocrite? Is that a word you call people who do things you don't want to do—like go to church? Is it a club used to clobber people we don't like? Or is it another way of using labels to keep from having to take each person on his own merit?

Our Lord taught so much about it that a definition is easily discovered. A hypocrite is several things. He is, first of all, someone who pretends he is better than he really is. Jesus found a lot of folks like this in the church of his day. I am sure he knows where some are in today's church. These are people who outwardly sing "To God Be the Glory" while inwardly saying "So long as I can get the credit."

Our text, from the Sermon on the Mount, stated that a hypocrite is one who does good deeds to be seen. When he prays, he does it only publicly, proudly, and to impress others.

There are many hypocrites outside the church. I knew a man who was not a Christian. He was reputed to be one of the best men in the community. He worked hard and provided well for his family. He loved his wife and children, and they were devoted to him. His honesty was known and appreciated by all. I visited him several times. Each time I would show him the Bible verse: "For all have sinned, and come short of the glory of God" (Rom. 3:23).

"I don't need that," he would say. "I am not a sinner. I am as good or better than anyone in your church." We never got any farther on any visit. But God planted that verse in his heart, and his great love convicted that man. One evening he came walking down an aisle to ask Jesus to forgive him of his sins. Every time I heard him pray after that, he would enthusiastically thank God for forgiving him of his sins. He admitted he had been kidding himself all those years before. He compared himself to others and acted as though he did not need to repent and come to Christ. Perhaps the biggest hypocrite of all is the one who says, "I don't need the church or what it has to offer. Let those who need that sort of thing go if they want. But I am above all that."

An Andy Capp cartoon showed Andy and Flo walking to church. Just beyond the church, Andy saw a pub, and the thought bubble above him indicated his desire for a beer. As they got to the church door, Andy did not turn in. Walking straight on, he piously said: "Too many hypocrites in there." Whereupon, his wife grabbed his arm, pulled him in and said: "One more won't hurt."

Some hypocrites do not pretend they are better than they are—instead they pretend they are worse than they really are. They claim to be wild, lewd, unbelieving, unconcerned, and uncommitted. Yet, they often pray and even have moments when they sincerely worship God.

Oscar Wilde, in the play *The Importance of Being Earnest* wrote: "I hope you have not been leading a double life, pretending to be wicked and really being good

. . . that would be hypocrisy." It is not difficult in our society to find hypocrites on both sides of the stained glass.

Another sin of pretense is to act as though we are stronger than we really are. In 1958, my daddy died suddenly and unexpectedly. I felt shocked, hurt, and sad. I kept thinking that since I am a Christian, and especially a preacher, I was supposed to be strong. I was amazed at the strength and grace God gave, and I was tempted to act stronger than I really was. The greatest ministry to me in those days was that neither my wife, my mother, our family pastor, nor any of my friends made me feel obligated to act stronger than I really was.

There are many facets of hypocrisy. To act better or worse, stronger or weaker than we really are, are some of the symptoms. Jesus said hypocrites are like cups which have been washed shiny and spotless on the outside, yet are filthy on the inside. A hypocrite is simply someone who pretends he is something he is not.

Then we are all hypocrites, aren't we? Oh, some are more hypocritical than others. Some sensitive souls are more aware of their hypocrisy than others who have formed thick callouses on their souls. But we all have the disease. Let that one who thinks he is without hypocrisy cast the first groan, for all of us, in varying degrees, are hypocrites.

How do we handle the hypocrite in us? Face up to it. Reading the Bible, we discover it to be one exposé or unmasking after another. Adam and Eve in the Garden of Eden had to be pushed out of their hiding. David was confronted by God's prophet after his affair with Bathsheba. "Thou art the man," he was told (2 Sam. 12:7). We read how people like you and I came to face themselves, got honest with themselves, and stopped trying to fool others and God. They took this first step toward release from phoniness.

The Bible is crammed full of flesh and blood examples

of weaknesses admitted and overcome. There was an uncouth fisherman named Peter, a despised tax collector called Matthew, and a woman of the streets named Mary. Read of a hateful, vengeful, sick little man called Saul of Tarsus who met Christ and became Paul the apostle and went about the pagan world happily declaring: "I know whom I have believed!" (2 Tim. 1:12).

In a hospital room I talked to a man about his splendid handling of a handicap—whereupon he delivered an eloquent lecture on the law of compensation, declaring his faith in the fact that handicaps can be turned into assets. The most afflicted of all people is that one who is handicapped spiritually, who has never faced up to his sins, turned himself in, and stood humbly before God to plead guilty and ask for his mercy. It is a great handicap to go through life pretending we don't need God's mercy and daily help.

We can never handle the hypocrite in us until we face up to it, come before God, and say, "Lord, I know I can't fool you anyway. I just thought I could sweep all that dirt under the floor, and you wouldn't see it. Let's get it out and look at it." And as you and God look at all the things you are ashamed of, so ashamed of, you say, "I am unworthy." Then you begin to learn how much God really loves you, and he says something like, "Relax, I do love you. I'm not going to throw you away. We can make something good out of this life. You are my son. You are my daughter." At this moment we understand what the Bible means by "grace."

But there is more. Those of us who have accepted his grace still have to struggle with hypocrisy.

You may be one of those sensitive persons who wonders about your motives for even the best things you do—like the teenage girl who wrote from camp: "I like the kids here very much. I enjoy being their friend. But I keep wondering if I am being friendly with them so maybe they'll elect me Camp President."

Sometimes we have to admit we don't know whether we are hypocrites or not. John Milton said we can't fully know. He wrote: "Neither man nor angel can discern hypocrisy, the only evil that walks invisible except to God alone."

For instance, I honestly do not know all my motives for wanting to preach the best sermons I can deliver each week. I know that preaching is God's will for my life. I am convinced he put me here to preach his Word. I am almost frightened each week at the thought of people watching and listening for some sure word from him. These alone are more than incentive enough. Yet there are other factors. The support and welfare of my family is at stake. Many listeners are complimentary, and it is always nice to get those verbal strokes. I sincerely pray each week about this very thing, asking God not only to help me preach, but to help me preach his Word for the right reasons. Yet, I don't think we will ever be able to know ourselves and all our motives. Our best prayers will simply ask him to help us do our best and to do what we do to honor him.

Dietrich Bonhoeffer was a great Christian if there ever was one. Even though it cost him his life, he would neither yield to Hitler's lies nor run from Hitler's power. While many German Christians who did not believe in Hitler's Nazism left the country, Bonhoeffer did not. He said: "I will not have the right to preach to my people when the war is over if I do not suffer with them through it."[1] So he spent the last years of his life in Hitler's concentration camps. He became a symbol of courage to other Christians. They loved and praised him. Much of their praise got back to him.

Out of that great man's Christian heart came some statements which have encouraged me more than anything I have read outside the Word of God. He spoke of knowing himself to appear confident to others, yet full of fear in his heart. The last lines of his long discourse state: "Who am I? They mock me, these lonely questions of mine. Whoever I am, Thou knowest, O God, I am Thine!"

Note

1. From *Letters and Papers from Prison.*

12

The Dust and the Deity
Matthew 6:19-24

He did not come to impose a burden on men. He came to lift men's burdens from them. He did not come to take away the joy of life. He came to instill joy into life.

There is one supreme fact about Christ we often overlook. He did not come to impose a burden on men. He came to lift men's burdens from them. He did not come to take away the joy of life. He came to instill joy into life. Too many times, in this age of guided missiles and misguided men, Christ has been taken to be a cosmic killjoy, a sort of resident policeman who raps our knuckles when we appear to be enjoying life. Before you fall for this satanic slander, let me remind you that Christ said, "I am come that they might have life . . . and have it more abundantly" (John 10:10).

In the Sermon of the Mount, Christ summed up the living of the Christian life, and the opening word, the keynote of this Magna Charta of the Kingdom of God, is the word *blessed*. And *blessed* means "happy." Do you see it? Christ has always said it; thousands have discovered it—the way of Christ is the blessed way, the happy way.

Beginning with verse 19 of the sixth chapter of Matthew, Jesus speaks of a matter relevant to all of us. He says that in this abundant way of life, we need to know how to deal with material riches. Both the having of money, and the lack of enough money, may have caused as much heartbreak as any other thing. So great an obstacle to the blessed life is this, that well over a third of all Christ had to say dealt with the subject.

Every Christian is a citizen of two worlds. And those worlds are so different! In our best moments, we know that both worlds, then and now, are to be committed to him and that Christian consistency commands commitment of every part of our lives.

So there comes a time when a follower of Christ must ask: "How do I feel about things? If I love Christ, how do I feel about my car? If he is my Master, how do I treat my money? I know I'm not supposed to love things and worship them. Does this mean I have to hate things and spurn them?"

This is not a question with an easy, pat, glib answer. We know we are made in God's image; thus we are spiritual. Also we are aware of being made of earth, to live on earth, so we are material. How do you reconcile dust and deity? How can we cope with being both material and spiritual? Each Christian struggles with the question: "How in heaven's name do I treat earth's things?"

So in his sermon on the happy, abundant way of life, Jesus speaks to us about the passion for possession, the principles of possessing, and the position of priority.

Hear him as he recognizes the passion for possession. We have to keep reminding ourselves, don't we, that we are creatures made by God. This means that, basically, we are as God made us. Now don't misunderstand. I am not saying we are as God meant us to be. We are not, because every man's life has been perverted by sin. Here is what I am saying, we have God-given instincts, but sin has perverted these drives and desires.

For instance, how about one of the major cracks in our culture today: the inordinate, unnatural obsession with sex. This is simply a case where Satan has been allowed to take a God-given desire and blow it all out of proportion until it is perverted.

Or take the matter of gambling, the foolish, often addictive way by which Satan erodes the character of a man. Said the poet,

> Some men die by shrapnel,
> And some go down in flames,

> But most men perish inch by inch
> Who play at little games. (Author unknown)

Yet we have this instinct for enterprise, the perversion of which is to gamble. God wants us to place our lives in his hands by faith, in order that we may fulfill this instinct for enterprise, this desire for real adventure.

The same is true of drinking and drugs. Every man has a hunger in his heart that merely living out his days in animal-like fashion cannot fulfill. This is the hunger that only God can satisfy. But Satan perverts this desire and leads many a misguided soul to seek refuge in a bottle, a pill, or needle, only to find greater distress. The Bible states, "And do not get drunk with wine, . . . but be filled with the Spirit" (Eph. 5:18, NASB). When men have God in their hearts, they do not need these demeaning crutches.

Just like every other drive and desire is God-given, though sin-perverted, even so is the passion for possession. Too many times we read where Christ said, "Lay not up for yourselves treasures upon earth," and forget that he said in the next verse, "But lay up for yourselves treasures in heaven" (Matt. 6:19-20). It is not the passion that is wrong. It is the perversion that is sinful. Here then we see what Christ is getting at—passion for possession without principle is perilous. Just as every source of energy and power must be bridled and guided, even so must be this desire to have. Our loving Lord is stating, "I want you to have; I want you to possess; I made you that way, but I want you to possess the best."

In verses 19 through 21 of Matthew 6, Christ presents Christian principles of possessing. The first is this: Temporary holdings do not constitute real riches. That which can be lost is not really owned. No man is rich to whom the grave brings bankruptcy.

I heard a man from Latvia tell what happened when the Communists took over. He was a member of a vastly wealthy family. Their chief holding was a giant city department store. "The day the Communists came," he said, "we were able to take out of the store only the clothes we were wearing. We left everything we owned in Latvia and fled for our freedom."

Here our Lord says (and I paraphrase),

> Because I love you, I do not want you to spend your short but valuable lives piling up temporary treasure. Haven't you lived long enough to observe that just about the time a man says, "I've got it made" that time runs out on him? Don't you know that earth's treasures are always being eaten by moths of depreciation, wasted by the rust of inflation, and stolen by the thousand and one variety of thieves that inhabit this earth?

Why don't we listen to Christ when he asks this pertinent question: "For what is a man profited, if he shall gain the whole world and lose his own soul?" (Matt. 16:26).

Here is the second principle: Eternal investment is wisest. "But lay up for yourselves treasures in heaven." God wants us to possess; he wants us to have; but he wants us to have the best. If you make your fortune on earth, you have made a fortune and stored it in a place where you cannot hold it. Make your fortune, but store it in a place where you can keep it, invest it in the Kingdom of God, and let it draw interest, compounded through eternity.

It should be crystal clear to us that Christ is talking about material wealth. He is not speaking of prayers you store up in heaven, or work you do for which you shall be rewarded. Here he is speaking of money.

Now why all this urgency? Why all this musing about so mundane a matter as money? Here is the third principle: We always look after our investments. "For where your treasure is, there will your heart be also" (Matt. 6:21). You see, your treasure itself is not of greatest importance. But what it does to your heart is important. This is why the love of money is called a "root of all sorts of evil" (1 Tim. 6:10, NASB). It can pull you down to a low level and change your life into a frustration of anxiety where your every desire, every joy, and every mood is directly related to the condition of the market and your bank account. But if invested in heaven, it can anchor your soul, fix your attention on the eternal, and keep your heart in the condition God wants it—and bring you happiness.

At this point, Christ seeks to impart to us the urgency of a right relation to the material by discussing two kinds of vision. He speaks of a "single eye" (Matt. 6:22) and an "evil eye" (Matt. 6:23). We must have a true view. A single eye is that vision which is unified. Thus, both eyes are singularly focused. The word *evil* means "out of order." If your vision of material goods is out of order, then your whole body is full of darkness. You are seeing falsely, and this is worse than being blind. A man who cannot see will be most careful so that he will not run into the ditch. But if the ditch looks like the road and the road looks like the ditch to him, then he will have great difficulty.

Far, far too many are suffering from a view of life that is completely out of order. Roy McLain said in a sermon:

> Perhaps the most ironical commentary on our civilization is that we are living on earth as though this were heaven and regarding heaven as though it were earth. We treat time as eternity and regard eternity as though it were the brief digit of time.

Don't get in the habit of laying up treasures on earth, because your heart will be there. You must look after your investments—that is the lesson. Your eye will be on your treasure, and happy is the day when the treasure pulls the eye into the gaze of heaven.

The principles of possessing are needful because God

demands the position of priority. "No man can serve two masters . . . . Ye cannot serve God and mammon" (Matt. 6:24). Here is the deepest thing of all. We have this passion to possess. What will we do with it? We will do with it what we do with any passion. We will worship with it. We may worship God with it, or we may worship mammon with it. But we cannot worship both God and money. That is the whole point. No man can become the slave of his treasure and worship it without thereby proving himself a traitor to God. No man can be a bond servant of God, worshiping him with all the heart, and still be enslaved by money.

Segregation can be, indeed, an ugly word. There is a kind of segregation more sinful than racial segregation. This is an approach to life which partitions our lives, like the pigeonholes in an old-fashioned rolltop desk. When you think religion and business are different matters, when you are offended at the idea that your faith may have something to say about how you get and use your income, when you assume that money management is not included in God's area of operation, when you lock him up in church and press him into the Bible like some faded rose leaf, then, my friend, it is time for you to know—and that right well—he is the Lord of the warehouse as well as the worship service. It is time for you to search a seldom-dusted corner of God's Word in Deuteronomy 8:18, and hear it loud and clear: "But you shall remember the Lord your God, for it is He who is giving you power to make wealth" (NASB).

Jesus did not ask every wealthy man he met to sell all his goods and give to the poor. When he did ask a man to do that, it was apparent that man thought he owned his things when really his things owned him. Our Lord was trying to free him from a cruel master (Luke 18:18-27).

A close study of Jesus' teachings indicates that the church has been presenting the wrong primary reasons for giving. Or as a favorite English teacher would say, "placing the emphasis on the wrong syllable." We have stressed the importance of separating you from your money because of what can be done with the money, and this is important. So many life and death ministries are involved. But the real concern should be you and the constant danger that your things may become your god. As you give part of your time, your toil and yourself, which is all money is, you are avoiding this danger.

A radiantly happy woman was asked the secret of her success in life. She answered: "I have never allowed the dollar bill to get bigger than my God."

The Old Testament commands, "Honour the Lord with thy substance" (Prov. 3:9). The New Testament tells us how to honor the Lord with our substance: "Upon the first day of the week let every one of you lay by him in store, as God hath prospered him" (1 Cor. 16:2). This is giving born not of whim, or of impulse, but of a steady orderliness sustained by your love for the Lord who gives you the power to get wealth, and your own determination that money will be your servant, not your god.

"No man can serve two masters . . . . You cannot serve God and money" (Matt. 6:24, author's words).

13

A Bad Man's Good Example
Luke 16:1-13

Day by day they appropriate the things of God—his air, his sunshine, his food, everything they have, and use them for selfish purposes. Actually they embezzle a life, because they give nothing in return. In building their lives, every single brick, tile, screw, and nail is stolen!

Hebrews 9:27 declares, "It is appointed unto men once to die, but after this the judgment." For many, that judgment will be a trial for embezzling. Several years ago, in *Beam* magazine, I read Paul Steven's report of a strange thief in Hamburg, Germany. There was not a single brick, tile, screw, or nail in his neat little house that had not been stolen. Over a period of two years and by way of eighty different thefts, the man accumulated every square inch of his house at someone else's expense. He even admitted he had stolen the flowers blooming in his front yard.

Day by day, bit by bit, he accomplished his theft. His actions parallel the spiritually criminal behavior of many men and women. Day by day they appropriate the things of God—his air, his sunshine, his food, everything they have—and use them for selfish purposes. Actually they embezzle a life, because they give nothing in return. In building their lives, every single brick, tile, screw, and nail is stolen!

You remember the well-traveled tale told by Edwin Markham: A wealthy man assigned a contractor to build a beautiful home. When plans and specifications were agreed upon, the rich man left on an extended trip. The builder, with no one around to check on him, proceeded to cheat on every specification of the house. Floors, beams, walls, and roof were of the cheapest material, all built on a flimsy and poorly built foundation.

When the rich man returned, he sought out the builder and said: "Here are the keys to the house—your house. You did not know it, but you built this home for yourself."

A constant warning from God's Word is that people who embezzle their lives from God are stuck with what they stole—a flimsy, deteriorating life dedicated to taking without ever making a payment.

A wrong handling of whatever wealth God has given to your care is subject to divine embezzling charges. Listen: "Will a man rob God? Yet you are robbing Me! But you say, 'How have we robbed Thee?' In tithes and contributions. You are cursed with a curse, for you are robbing Me" (Mal. 3:8-9, NASB).

Those are heavy words, yet they are underscored by the teaching of our Lord. He had more to say about this than about prayer, for you cannot pray to God while worshiping money.

Among the many things our Lord said about our handling of money, facing a divine audit, is a puzzling parable about a bad man's good example. Our Lord told his disciples this story about a rich fellow who had a steward, a business manager, who looked after his vast holdings. One day he discovered this business manager was cheating on him, stealing from him. He called the fellow on the carpet; let him know he was wise to his dark dealings; and fired him, giving him a few days to settle his affairs and put the books in order.

In wide-eyed panic, this dishonest dealer began to ponder his future. "What in the world am I going to do? I'm too lazy to work. I'm too proud to beg. What in the world will I do?" The wheels in his brain began to turn. Of course, they turned in the wrong direction. That's the only way they knew how to turn. Greased by greed, they turned swiftly and at last he said, "I've got it! I'll call in my boss's debtors and reduce their debts, falsifying their accounts. Then, because I've helped them, they will feel obligated to help me. And, if they don't feel obligated enough, I'll have something to blackmail them with because they had a part in the crime." So he called them in:

"How much do you owe my boss?"

"One hundred measures of oil."

"Then change it to fifty," he said.

He asked another, "What is your debt?"

"One hundred measures of wheat."

He instructed him, "Then write down eighty." He must not have liked that fellow as much.

Well, the boss, of course, discovered this trickery, too. Having pulled a few shady deals himself, he could not help admiring the act a little, but he didn't let him get by with it. Jesus said, in effect, "Now that fellow is smarter in the things of this world than a lot of you are in the things of the Spirit."

One of our biggest problems in studying parables in the Bible is that we are tempted to milk as many teachings out of them as we can squeeze. We try to make them crawl on all fours, when really Jesus told a story for the same reason you and I would tell a story, to illustrate one truth.

Here is all our Lord was saying: This man knew his income was soon to be gone, so he made provision for income when that happened. We know that soon our lives on this earth will be ended. For almost everyone, the end comes much sooner than we expect. Then why don't we make provision for that?

You are going to outlive your income. You, my friend, are eternal. You are going to live forever. On the other hand, your wealth is temporary. Luke 16:9 is instructing you to invest your wealth in such a way that when it fails, or is worth nothing, you will have a place in eternal dwelling places.

Now, you ought to be thinking about that, making preparations for that. This parable is saying what we all know to be true. This world is not enough. There is a cemetery in every town to remind us of this.

Remember the story of two men who were discussing a wealthy man's death? One asked, "How much did he leave?" To which the other replied, "He left it all."

The old Chinese proverb is true: "There are no pockets in a shroud." The not-so-old preacher's proverb is also true: "There are no U-haul trailers behind hearses." You cannot take it with you.

"Their inward thought is," said the Psalmist, "that their houses shall continue for ever, and their dwelling places to all generations; they call their lands after their own names" (Ps. 49:11). That is sheer mockery! "For," as the Psalmist says of one who lusts after the treasures of earth, "when he dieth he shall carry nothing away" (Ps. 49:17).

Alexander the Great was born to one empire and conquered another. He possessed the wealth of both the East and the West. Yet he commanded that when carried to his grave his hands should be left unwrapped and outside the bier so that all might see them empty.

The Great Charlemagne was, at his request, buried sitting on his throne, wearing his crown, robe, and jewels. In his lap was an open Bible and his lead finger was resting on Mark 8:36, "For what does it profit a man to gain the whole world, and forfeit his soul?" (NASB).

In the incident recorded in the twelfth chapter of Luke, Jesus was sharing some extremely heavy thoughts with his listeners. One man in the crowd was apparently not hearing a word. Suddenly he blurted: "Master, would you talk to my brother? Tell him to divide the inheritance with me" (see v. 13).

I wonder if right now you can't really worship God because you are preoccupied with money—how to get it or how to keep from losing it. Someone you know may have so much you're thinking: "I wish he or she would give me some." It is possible to think about money so much you don't think of anything else. Our Lord's word to that young man and to you and me is, "Beware, and be on your guard against every form of greed" (Luke 12:15, NASB).

He never makes a statement without giving a reason. Why shouldn't we be greedy? Why not get all we can? That's how the system works, isn't it?

Here is his answer in that same verse: "For not even when one has an abundance does his life consist of his possessions" (NASB). How many of us really believe that when we ask how much is a man or woman worth? When we answer only in terms of wealth, aren't we saying: "No Jesus, you are wrong! Life does consist of the abundance of things possessed. It's the American dream to be rich. Why, some television preachers even say that's what you meant by the 'abundant life.' "

Our Lord is very anxious for us to understand exactly what he is saying, so the Master Teacher followed his statement with a story. You've heard it before, probably. It's the story of a successful farmer who one day surveyed his fields and determined he had the prospect of the greatest harvest ever. Even without the aid of a pocket calculator, he rightly reasoned he had inadequate storage facilities for such a bumper crop. Such a problem was hardly a challenge to this enterprising gentleman. He decided to tear down his present facilities and build a larger one. Later, the ecstasy of that bumper crop in the field and that big beautiful barn being built caused him to exclaim: "My soul, I have it made! At last I am secure. No more days of work, nor long nights of worry. I can eat, drink, and sleep now. I have arrived!"

What would you call such a man? What do you call such people? Why, they're all around you. You see them at the country club, the bank, and in the stores. How do you see them? Do you call them "prudent," "sharp," or "successful"?

Jesus called the man a fool. And so he was. In fact, he could only become a bigger fool if he gained weight!

He was not foolish because he was successful. He was foolish because he was a failure. God said, in effect, "You are a fool because you are only rich in this world. You will be a pauper in the next. No one can be counted wise or successful who could have had a mansion in heaven and ends up in a mud hut in hell."

Now hear this: God's Word clearly declares that though you can't take what you've greedily grasped with you, you can send what you've cheerfully given on ahead. Luke 16:9-12 presents this fact. In the Sermon on the Mount, Jesus declared: "Lay up for yourselves treasures in heaven" (Matt. 6:20).

When you go to a foreign country, you usually have to exchange currency. You can't use Canadian quarters in Chicago's soft drink machines. I believe our Lord is telling us we can deposit treasure to our account in heaven. All of this is based on God's command to tithe and to go beyond that in giving offerings. He desires to share his love and save from their sin as many as will come to him. We are all commanded to be part of that. As we invest in that venture, we are laying up treasure in heaven.

One way to determine your sense of values is to inventory your investments. If you are piling up treasure which is only of this world, you have judged yourself. You are a one-world person. When this life is over, you will be a pauper. If you are investing in the kingdom of God, your sense of eternal values is revealed.

I once was pastor of a church the people of the city called "The First National Baptist Church." I recoil at any tag which takes away a sense of family and hints at institution. But there is a real sense in which a church is like a bank. All the tithes and offerings you and I have been bringing to church are transactions of heavenly business. We have been exchanging treasure we can't keep for wealth we can't lose.

14

When You Can't Slay the
Giants Anymore
2 Samuel 21:15-22

It could be the best day of your life is the day
you learn you can't slay all the giants.

It could be the best day of your life is the day you learn you can't slay all the giants. You remember how the Word of God tells of David slaying the giant Goliath when David was very young and had great faith in God. Well, on a different day, he confidently went forth to do battle with another giant.

All of us face giants in our daily living. A long list could be made. There is a habit you started in your younger, greener days. You knew the giant had felled many another, but you were sure you could take him. And now you have become painfully aware that you can't slay the giant anymore. Perhaps it is some goal, some success, a noble achievement for which you aspired. Something you knew would be hard, but you set out confidently to overcome, has now become more of a challenge than you thought. It's a hard thing to face up to the fact that you are not a giant killer, after all. And yet, at a time when all looks lost, when the giant you set out to conquer stands poised powerfully over you about to strike the death blow, it just might be your best hour.

The day you learn you can't slay all the giants is the day you learn to identify your real enemy. David was jeopardizing his future and the future of all who depended on him by proudly assuming a strength and ability he didn't possess. He had gone against Goliath with confidence in God, but he faced Goliath's brother with confidence in David.

The Bible warns us against trusting ourselves and

"leaning to our own understanding" (see Prov. 3:5). We have an enemy whose avowed purpose is to trick us into personal and eternal destruction. One day God said to Satan, "Have you considered my servant Job?" (see Job 1:8). My, what an interesting word *considered* is. It describes an enemy patiently watching, looking for your weakest link.

You remember Pogo? He's one of my favorite philosophers. He said, "We have met the enemy, and he is us." The Prodigal Son, pondering his problems, came to *himself*. And the day you learn you can't slay all the giants is when you finally learn that perhaps in yourself you have found your greatest enemy.

The day you learn you can't slay the giants is when you discover your enemies, but you can also discover your allies. Just as the giant was about to take David, Abishai came to his rescue. This could well be the first time David was aware that he was not fighting alone. Oh, he knew there were other people around doing battle, but I wonder if he had recognized the fact that he needed them? Fellowship's largest lesson is learned not from the warm glow we get when we help others, but from that first difficult time when we have to accept help from others. We ought to be like C. D. Meigs who prayed:

> Lord, help me live from day to day
> In such a self-forgetful way,
> That even when I kneel to pray
> My prayer shall be for—Others.
> ("Others," *Broadman Hymnal* © 1940, p. 77)

We should pray with Francis of Assisi, "Make me an instrument of Thy peace." Yet I'm convinced we become much better instruments of fellowship after once we've been the object of the fellowship.

The swaggering, confident, benevolent, yet superior king lay on his back with that hulk of humanity about to strike the death blow. Then he was rescued. I am certain

David was a different man from that day.

In the Scripture we see him doing two things immediately. First, he avows in a fresh way, "The Lord is my rock, and my fortress, and my deliverer" (2 Sam. 22:2). And after that psalm is completed, he sets about to name the people who are so important to him, beginning in 2 Samuel 23:8. Those of us who know that we can't slay all of life's giants alone feel the same way. We need our friends.

Have you noticed how Alcoholics Anonymous has captured what it really means to be a church—a fellowship of God? In AA, you've got to say, "I've got a problem and I can't handle it, and I need God's help. And I need the help of other people who have the same problem." In the church we say, "Lord, I've got a problem. I'm a sinner, and I can't stop being a sinner. And I need God's help, but I also need the help of others who have the same problem." And that, friend, is what "fellowship" is all about.

Near the beginning of his little letter John says, "That which we have seen and heard declare we unto you, that ye also may have fellowship with us" (1 John 1:3). And our fellowship is with the Father and his son, Jesus Christ.

So much depends upon the kind of company you keep. If you are married, your marriage depends upon the social life you lead. If you are a Christian, your commitment depends on the company you keep. It's so for all of us.

We also need fellowship with the Father, through his son Jesus Christ. Our sin has separated us from him, and God is saying, "I love you. I miss you. I want to bring joy and peace to your life." Christ came down here to pay a great price. He defeated the two giants about to snuff us out . . . *sin* and *death.* We learn to really live on that good day when we realize how much we need him and need each other.

15

How to Say "Thy Will Be Done"
Matthew 26:36-39

It is my conviction this picture of grief and victory in a garden is more than sacred history. It is also our Lord declaring, "Let me teach you how to say: 'Thy will be done!' "

We must never forget that Jesus Christ was a man as well as God. His life is a perfect picture of how a human being is to face this world. We have let Satan dupe us into thinking that since Jesus was God, somehow that last terrible week of his earthly life was easier for him. "Not so!" proclaims God's Word.

When we see him facing with quiet calmness the injustices of the soldiers and authorities, as we watch him hoist the hideous log on which he is to be executed and half carry, half drag it out to Golgotha, at least as far as his battered and beaten body can manage, looking at him hanging there forgiving sins, seeing him caring for his mother and praying for his murderers, we are prompted to say, "That is so abnormal. He is not facing that with the difficulty of a man." One thing is wrong with an evaluation like that. It leaves out Gethsemane. It misses the fact that Jesus was not struggling with the cruelties of the cross, because he had already fought the battle at Gethsemane.

Gethsemane, an ancient word meaning "the oil press," was a garden spot, a place designed to enjoy the beauties of growing things. Jerusalem was built on the top of Mount Zion. There was no place for gardens or yards. So the wealthy people had their gardens on the slopes of the Mount of Olives. They were reached by descending from Jerusalem into the ravine, through which the brook Kidron flowed, and then climbing the slopes of the hill on the other side. This particular spot probably belonged to some friend who allowed Jesus to use it as he wished. John 18:2 asserts that Jesus went there often.

In this place of solitary agony, our blessed Lord fought this last battle with Satan. It was awesome and terrible. The Word asserts that horror and dismay came over him. "The sorrow in my heart is so great that it almost crushes me" (Matt. 26:38, TEV), he said.

Gethsemane was far more terrible than Calvary. We are not able to understand the depths of the agony in the garden. We dare not try to explore the anguish of heart which forced our Savior to exclaim: "My soul is deeply grieved, to the point of death" (Matt. 26:38, NASB). We do know that in the face of overwhelming waves of spiritual and physical anguish, he won the victory and said: "Yet not as I will, but as Thou wilt" (Matt. 26:39, NASB).

My conviction is that this picture of grief and victory in a garden is more than sacred history. It is also our Lord stating, "Let me teach you how to say: 'Thy will be done!' "

We must begin with a commitment to God's will concerning our salvation and our lives. Jesus had made a commitment to God's plan for our salvation and God's will for his life prior to this time. As a twelve-year-old boy, he had said: "I must be about my Father's business" (Luke 2:49). When he was baptized by John the Baptist, he was graphically and symbolically declaring his commitment to the will of his Father. In the temptation experience in the wilderness, Christ struggled with God's will and chose the way of the cross and its difficulty rather than the flashier, crowd-pleasing, circus-type, ministry Satan offered him.

Our Lord had faced and deliberately made these decisions and was so committed to his Father's way that even the Calvary kind of death, as terrible as it was, was not nearly so bad as missing God's will for his life.

The Bible plainly states that you and I are to make

similar commitments. Satan tempted Jesus, saying: "You don't have to die on a cross, just help the people. Treat them nicely, heal their bodies, feed them bread, and entertain them with magical tricks. But don't die on a cross." That same Satan says to you and me: "You don't need anything that drastic to forgive your sins. Sure, you're not perfect. But who is? Just do the best you can."

Christ successfully resisted those subtle temptations, and so must we. It does take the cross to pay for our sins. Our Lord knew that, so he died on the cross for us. We know it, so we come to that cross for salvation.

And we come to that cross not only with a plea for forgiveness, but with a presentation of our lives. No one ever experiences the thrill of discipleship until he asserts: "I am yours, Lord. I want your will to be done in this life."

Herein lies the difference between the shallow emotionalism of people in search of spiritual kicks and the steady, dependable soldier of the cross. There is a vast difference between staging exciting spiritual pep rallies and fielding a good strong team.

Now there is nothing wrong with pep rallies. They help. Pep rallies can be giant successes on just the emotion of the moment. But the game is won or lost on the basis of commitment to the task. You can have a good pep rally with a gifted and charismatic cheerleader, but you can't have a good team unless there is dedication and preparation, effort and desire, on the part of the members of that team.

One can walk into a pep rally, having paid no price in preparation, out-of-shape, maybe not even knowing what the school colors are, and soon get caught up in the cheers and noise of the moment. But a team cannot simply walk on the field the day of the game and decide to win. That decision had to be made long before and backed up by many an act of personal and collective discipline.

So it is in pleasing God. You do not inherit eternal riches, and you do not win in life's game by attending an occasional pep rally and giving a resounding three cheers for Jesus.

You must allow yourself to come under the discipline of the Coach who said: "If any man will come after me, let him deny himself, take up his cross daily, and follow me" (Luke 9:23). We must not picture ourselves as spectators perched comfortably in the stands, thinking that since we bought our tickets we have the right to let others throw the blocks and run with the ball.

When we have made this commitment, we strive to keep it current. The New Testament is interspersed with accounts of our Lord's habit of withdrawing to a quiet place and praying to his Heavenly Father. John tells us Jesus came to Gethsemane quite often for this purpose. His prayer was always: "Thy will be done."

When you and I learn to pray we begin to see that effective prayer is not measured by how much you can get out of God, but by how much of God we let into our daily living. Only this continuing commitment to the way of the Father prepares us for the times when we are called to bear an unbearable cross.

Simon Peter, James, and John went with him into that garden. It had been a long, puzzling, and stress-filled week. They were exhausted emotionally and physically, so they slept in spite of his pleas for their prayer support while he fought the battle alone. When he woke them and together they faced the mob that had come to arrest Jesus, they simply were not prepared. Simon Peter took out his sword and tried to fight. James, John, and the rest of the apostles turned and fled into the darkness. Yet Jesus faced that mob as though he were arresting them. His quiet dignity in the midst of gross indignity amazed everyone, especially Pilate. The apostles were not prepared for that hour, so they acted from shocked impulse. On the other hand, Jesus had prepared, and he was oper-

ating in the calm confidence of the Father's will. Gethsemane for Jesus was not a retreat. It was a preparation
for attack. He did not go to hide from death. He went to
prepare for it.

Only those who have already committed themselves to
the Father's will consistently win the battles against
Satan. The Christian young person must make decisions
concerning personal purity and integrity in some Gethsemane experience, not during the passion of temptation.
The Christian husband or wife will need to settle the
"Thy will be done" in a time of personal commitment,
not when the office hedonist leads the enticing discus-
sions about the freedom of the new morality. A businessman's integrity is settled in his continuing commitment,
not when the temptation of the easy, dishonest dollar is
dangled before his eyes.

You will never be able to successfully come through
your Golgotha experience until you have first been to
Gethsemane. Like Jesus, you will probably have to go
alone. He took his friends part of the way, but they were
so physically exhausted and emotionally drained that
sleep overcame them. In Gethsemane times friends are
seldom a help. Certain things have to be settled in the
loneliness of your own soul and in fellowship with God.

If some Gethsemane experience for you has been a
crushing thing you could not understand; if the heart in
you has ever asked, "Why?"; then you can know an
understanding heart beats in the breast of our Savior. In
Gethsemane he, too, was asking "Why?" Am I too pre-
sumptuous in reading into our Lord's agony thoughts
like these:

> Father, does it have to come now? There are so few
> supporters. There is so little accomplished, and so
> much to do. The three best ones are out there sound
> asleep right now. Father, please let this cup pass
> from me; nevertheless, not my will but thine be
> done.

In that submission is the greatest lesson of all. It is not only that Jesus said: "Thy will be done," but the attitude in which he said it. The Bible makes it plain that one day every knee will bow and every tongue will confess that Jesus Christ is Lord (see Phil. 2:9-10). So in one way or another every creature on this earth will eventually be forced to say: "You are Lord. Your will is supreme."

But saving and winning commitment must come before that day. And it must come in an attitude of childlike trust. Mark 14:36 records that Jesus prayed: "Abba! Father! All things are possible for Thee; remove this cup from Me; yet not what I will, but what Thou wilt" (NASB).

Twice in the Greek language of the New Testament the Aramaic word *Abba* occurs. It is used in Gethsemane by Jesus and in Galatians by Paul. Both men grew up in homes where Aramaic was the household language, even though Greek was the universal tongue. *Abba* is the word a child used for his father. It is almost the same as our children saying "Daddy." I hope you catch the great thrust of that. Jesus is saying, "I do not understand all of this, but I am your child and I trust you."

I have known people who felt compelled to say "Lord, thy will be done" in broken, abject surrender. They supposed themselves to be beaten to their knees by a supreme God. So they gave up.

Others have said "Thy will be done" in weary resignation—as ones who struggle and fight, and finally decide that further resistence is useless. So they hopelessly give in.

Many people have framed their submission to God's will in bitter resentment. They don't like it and can't do anything about it, so like a rebellious child they just give in begrudgingly to it.

In this holy experience, Jesus shows us that the words are to be spoken in love and trust. We do not need to understand in order to submit. We know the Father's hand will never cause his child a needless tear. We can

see ourselves not as playthings of circumstance, or victims of blind tyranny, but much loved children in the
hands of a Heavenly Father.

From our place of commitment, we can march out to
meet whatever attack Satan directs at us. In calm confidence, our hearts can sing: "I know not what the future
holds, but I know who holds the future."

Reading through the Bible, you get the idea that God
has an affinity for beautiful gardens. In the second
chapter of the Bible we are told he created a garden
called Eden for his people to enjoy. But sin befouled that
beautiful picture of perfection and has taken the joy of
that God-intended bliss away from us. In the last
chapter of the Bible God promises for his people another
garden—a perfect place to live forever as God originally
intended. But it is in Gethsemane, this garden in the
middle of the Bible, that the final decision was made to
make it all possible for you and me. In Eden two people
said, in effect, "Not thy will, but mine be done." Because
you and I have said the same thing, we have forfeited our
right to fellowship with God. In the garden in the middle
of the Bible, Jesus said: "Not my will, but thine be
done," and he went out and paid the price for your sins
and mine.

You see, because God bought your pardon, he promises you more than a rose garden. He offers you forgiveness for all your sins. He offers you complete acceptance.
He offers you a salvation that begins the moment you accept it. It includes the strength you need to live here as
well as the promise of living hereafter. You enter into this
best kind of life that never ends by saying: "Not my way
of salvation, Lord, but yours. Not my life, but yours. Not
my will, but thine be done." Have you the courage and
the common sense to latch onto that?

16

You Don't Have to Doubt!
John 20:24-29

What do you do when faith falters? How do you keep faith's reserves in readiness for unavoidable times when life tumbles in, if your disposition is such that you find it difficult to accept anything not seen or felt in the two-by-four dimensions of time and life?

In a speech that has taxed the memory of many a high school sophomore, Shakespeare had Mark Antony say, "The evil that men do lives after them;/The good is oft interred with their bones" (*Julius Caesar*, III, ii, 80-81).

Why is it that most of us are so quick to overlook the good things about a man, but recall in vivid, technicolor detail his mistakes?

Several years ago, a dazed football player ran the wrong way. Everywhere he goes that poor fellow is remembered as the man who ran the wrong way. Not a word is said about the hundreds of times he ran the right way. They just remember that he ran the wrong way once.

Arnold Palmer and Jack Nicklaus played an exhibition round of golf on our local course. It was a terrible day. On one occasion Mr. Palmer almost missed the ball completely. Every time you get close to that particular spot somebody will inevitably say, "Boy, ole' Palmer really chilly-dipped one over there."

In the eighth grade, my greatest claim to notoriety was the fact that I was offside on the play that would have been our only touchdown of the season! I was not allowed readily to forget this fact. "The evil that men do lives after them!"

Perhaps for this reason, the man who made the highest profession of faith in the Bible is remembered as "Doubting Thomas." He was a doubter, to be sure, but he defeated his doubts. His faith won out, and what we ought to remember is that he said, "My Lord and my God!" (John 20:28).

What do you do when faith falters? How do you keep faith's reserves in readiness for unavoidable times when life tumbles in, if your disposition is such that you find it difficult to accept anything not seen or felt in the two-by-four dimensions of life and time?

If these are the questions that beg for a hearing at the tribunal of your mind, then through the experience of Thomas, God has something to say to you.

First, consider what we know about Thomas. You may see something of yourself in this man. James states that the Word of God is like a mirror of the soul. You look in it, and you see yourself. If so, then know that God is speaking to your heart.

It is not my intention that we simply pick Thomas apart—as though studying the Bible were only an exercise in disecting ancient history. Indeed, it is just the opposite. The Word of God is as relevant as today's newspaper—with much more pertinent news. God would say to us, through the experience of Thomas, that doubts can be overcome; that faith, when assailed, can win; that it is possible for the same man who said, "I will not believe" (v. 25) to come to the point of saying "My Lord and my God."

The first biblical picture of Thomas shows him to be a daring realist. The situation had to do with the death and raising of Lazarus. At that time the apostles were already under the shadow of the Lord's approaching cross. They were greatly perplexed and profoundly conscious of the keen hostility against Jesus in Judea and especially Jerusalem. In recent days, Christ had narrowly escaped mobs who demanded his death by stoning. They were grateful to be out of that region and away from his enemies. Then word came from Mary and Martha that Lazarus was critically ill. Christ announced after two days that he would go to Judea, and they spoke of their fear for his life and begged him not to go. When it became apparent that Christ meant it, that he really was going, Thomas said, "Let us also go, that we may die with Him"(John 11:16, NASB).

In this statement, Thomas proved himself to be a pre-eminently practical man. He was sure that the Jews who wanted so much to kill Jesus would find a way to do so. He showed himself to be unswervingly loyal. He had made his decision to follow Jesus, and now he would stick with it even though it might cost him his life. He was an absolutely honest man. He did not think that they ought to go and was honest in saying so, but, none-theless, he would not desert his Master.

The second biblical picture we have of Thomas focuses even more sharply upon his absolute honesty. We find Jesus giving to his disciples those wonderful final instructions contained in chapters 13 through 17 of the Book of John. He was talking to them of his going, and after a discussion with the apostle Peter, he said: "And whither I go ye know, and the way ye know" (John 14:4). Then, again, the impulsive, honest voice of Thomas said, "Lord, we know not whither thou goest; and how can we know the way?" (John 14:5).

It was the language of honesty, the language of a man who would not allow a teacher to go on and take for granted things that were not so. They did not know the destination, so how could they know the way? Note that he said, "Lord." This means that still his unswerving loyalty to Christ had not slackened. How glad we are that he asked this question, for it is to this question of Thomas our Lord replied, "I am the way, the truth, and the life. . . ." (John 14:6). If Thomas had not asked the question, we may never have had these clarifying and comforting words from Christ.

The next account we have of Thomas takes place in the upper room after the resurrection. The disciples were again in the midst of mystery. Everything was changed. The shadow of the cross, which had plagued them, had ceased to be a shadow. It had become real and had brought about the death of their loved one. By that death they had been scattered, but by the news of the resurrection they had been regathered.

They were in an upper room, all except Thomas, when Christ appeared and proved his resurrection. The next day they told Thomas. He was sure they were victims of some hallucination. "It was impossible!" He blurted out, "Unless I see the scars and feel them, I will not believe." If we must place some blame on Thomas, let's not do it here. I think you and I would have reacted in the same way. If there is a criticism to be made, it is for his being absent from the first meeting. Still being absolutely honest, he declined to profess a faith he did not have. Much is to be said in favor of Thomas because he was in church on the next Sunday. He placed himself in the position of being blessed. Christ came, apparently for the sake of Thomas, because immediately after addressing the others he turned to Thomas and said: "Feel my wounds; see for yourself." And Thomas responded, "My Lord and my God."

In this case history from the Bible, God is telling anyone how to defeat his doubts. A primary requirement is that one be an honest doubter. There are many dishonest doubters. Some do not want to believe in God because they want to live ungodly lives. Others doubt the virtue of Christians because they choose not to be virtuous. Some question the honesty of other people because they themselves prefer to live by dishonest means. The dishonest doubter seems to thrive on doubt; he likes it, enjoys it, sports it, lives by it, goes around telling people about his doubts—as some morbid folk have a fancy for showing their scars and talking about their symptoms, as though everything that makes them different from others, even though it be a disease, were a thing to be proud of.

Thomas was not playing at mental gymnastics. He was no intellectual acrobat, turning flips of the mind just for the sport of it. He was a serious seeker of the truth.

Don't think of him as Doubting Thomas. Think of him as courageous, honest, seeking Thomas. Do not mistake him for the pseudointellectual whose only answer to faith is a sneer. This man wanted to know. So must be the attitude of any real seeker. Whatever the truth is, he must know.

We can only imagine what must have gone through Thomas's mind after the others told him about seeing Christ. He may have said to himself:

> *It is incredible to believe that he is alive. I saw his power and influence and strength disappear in those short dreadful days. He was utterly helpless before the mob that came after him. I have heard him, on many occasions, speak with such authority the wisest of the Pharisees had no answer for him. And yet, during that trumped-up trial, he had no defense for himself. He did not even speak one word. This same one had amazed us all by single-handedly and forcibly driving from the Temple all the money changers and merchants, using no weapon but a small cord. Yet, he took that cross and submitted to it without even flexing a muscle to avoid it. I was there when they hammered him to that hideous log. I heard the cry of despair from his lips, "My God, my God, why hast thou forsaken Me?" (Matt. 27:46). I watched that brutish soldier thrust a spear deep in his side. I saw the limp, bloodstained body taken down from the cross and placed in a borrowed tomb. I heard the hollow thud as they rolled the rock into place and observed them seal it up tight. My eyes did not deceive me. He was dead!*
>
> *Yet, strangely, a prophesy my mother used to*

*quote from the scroll of Isaiah has kept repeating it-
self to my mind, "He was bruised for our iniquities"
(Is. 53:5). John the Baptist introduced him to us as
the "Lamb of God, which taketh away the sin of
the world" (John 1:29). Was that cross God's way
of sacrificing his Son, like a Temple lamb, for the
sins of the world? Only a few days ago Jesus said,
"Destroy this temple, and in three days I will raise it
up" (John 2:19, NASB). Could it be that he was
talking of his body and not a building?*

*There is no doubt that he at least had power over
death. I saw him stop a funeral procession in Nain
and bring the widow's son back. When I thought
we would surely lose our lives with him when we
came back to Judea, I saw him go to a tomb and
bring out Lazarus—alive!*

*He could be alive. He really could. How I wish I
were able to believe like Peter. He never seems to
doubt anything, but I'm just not built like that. And
really, I'm not asking for any more proof than they
had. They said they saw him, and I must see, too, if
I am to believe.*

*If only I had been there last night. If I had been
with them, I would know now whether it were true
or not.*

*I must know. If it is true, I cannot miss it again. If
he really is alive, at least I'll put myself in the best
possible position to find out. I will stay with the
others. If he really is alive, surely he will come
again.*

Such could have been the thoughts of Thomas.

On the next Sunday evening, it happened. Christ suddenly appeared, and he said to Thomas, "See my hands?
Feel them. Feel my side. There, where the scar is." But
Thomas did not need to touch. He bowed himself in total
trust and said, "My Lord and my God."

Would you notice Thomas missed the first blessing because he was not in the fellowship of the saints, but received the certainty because he was with them the second time? Does this not say to us that certainty is most likely to come to us in the fellowship of believers? When Thomas was alone, he was doubly alone. He cut himself off from the fellowship of Jesus Christ. When he came back into that fellowship he met Christ again. Nowhere is one more likely to find Christ than in the company of those who love Christ.

There is another lesson here. When your faith is assailed, deal directly with Christ. It was in that manner that Thomas came to victory. If you would defeat your doubts, go to Christ for yourself. Get him for yourself. You may ask, "How can I do this? How can I find him?" I make the answer with strong conviction. Do away with all literature pro or con about Christ. Take as your only source the New Testament. Read the Book of John. I do not believe that anyone can honestly read these biblical stories, steep himself in them, make himself acquainted with the Christ presented there, and not come to say, "My Lord and my God." I pray that will be your happy experience!

In this Scripture, Christ presents his last beatitude: "Blessed are they that have not seen, and yet have believed" (John 20:29). This is the special blessing of God upon all who have trusted Christ through total faith. If your faith comes easy, be thankful for it. But wait patiently for Thomas, he will be along shortly. When he comes, his confession will lack nothing.

This last word to you on doubt: Stay with Christ's people, for it is here you most likely will find him. Find your way to Christ yourself—the Christ of the New Testament. Tell him all your doubts, fears, and griefs. And you will find him to be a living one speaking through his Word today as surely as he spoke to Thomas. And at last in him, and in him alone, will you find the rest you are seeking.

17

Having What It Takes
Psalm 62:7-8

Does he have what it takes to survive this? Is there enough inner strength to come through, or will he be crushed and defeated?

Eavesdropping is not my favorite hobby, but my scrambled egg had not gotten there yet, and the man at the next table was speaking in a loud, resonant, clear, clipped, and cold voice. If I understood correctly he was, on behalf of his employer, firing the man across the table from him. Immediately my attention was drawn to the greying, middle-aged man who had just had the rug pulled out from under him. My experience in counseling with men in this position made me wonder: *Does he have what it takes to survive this? Is there enough inner strength to come through, or will he be crushed and defeated? The attitude and love of his family and friends will play a large part.* I wondered about those who would be around him in the next few days, but most of all, I prayed: "O, Lord, may he have within him what it takes."

David had what it takes. God's Word tells us about it. David's life experiences before he became king would plot on a graph like the outline of a roller coaster. He was not the most respected member of his family. In fact, when Saul told Jesse he was going to ordain one of his sons as future king, Jesse did not even invite David to the meeting. It is pretty apparent he did not consider young David most likely to be crowned king, even in his family.

When David's great confidence in God led him to fight and win over Goliath, he became an instant national hero. This man's amazing character showed itself in sev-

120

eral ways. He did not become cocky or arrogant. He kept himself in apparent and careful obedience to the king. You can usually measure the maturity in men or women by watching how they relate to authority. Respect for authority is always a badge of true character. David did not become aloof and withdrawn. The people loved him because he was friendly. Don't you know that after the defeat of Goliath, he was asked to autograph the slingshot of every boy in Palestine? He must have been obliging, for the people loved him.

Yet, trouble came for David—unfair, cruel trouble. King Saul proved to be one of those people who got older but never grew up. He had broad shoulders but a narrow, jealous mind. He did not have the character to match his hulk.

For almost fourteen years, Saul made life for David a living hell. He would call David to play his harp, then go into a jealous rage and throw his spear at him. He tried to fix things so David would be killed in battle. He sent servants to David's house to kill him. This Old Testament version of the "Godfather" forced David to run for his life, to live like an animal in caves. He hunted David like a partridge (see 1 Sam. 26:20). He turned the people against him. Saul gave David's wife to another man. Finally, David had to live in exile with his enemies, the Philistines, as one disowned by his own people.

Through all this, David kept and increased his faith in God. He did not become vengeful. Twice he could have killed Saul, but he would not. He did not become bitter or rebellious. He did not pity himself.

He had a fantastic, unbelievable heart. One day David was having to run down one side of a mountain while Saul and his monstrous army were coming up the other side. They were not there to play "tag." They were intent on killing David. For years he faced, unjustly, that kind of pressure, yet he said: "Then I lay down and slept in peace and woke up safely, for the Lord was watching

over me. And now, although ten thousand enemies sur-
round me on every side, I am not afraid." Knowing his
experiences brings Psalm 23 to life, doesn't it? "Even
though I walk through the valley of the shadow of death,
I fear no evil; for Thou art with me . . . Thou dost prepare a table before me in the presence of my enemies" (Ps.
23:4-5, NASB).

How we need that! How do we get that? Just like
David. He was no superman. His later sins show us that.
He was just what you and I can be—a simple man with
a super God!

Anyone who has what it takes will have a relationship
with God. He will not merely believe in God. He will not
just have great respect for God. He will love God. One
thing you just cannot miss in the life of David was his
love for his God.

Oh, how that is missing today! Many are the foolish
folk who will try to use God. Some highly respect God,
much like a visiting dignitary. But the one who has a
right relationship with him will love him. His prayers
will sound somewhat like David's prayers: "Bless the
Lord, O my soul: and all that is within me, bless his holy
name" (Ps. 103:1). "My flesh and my heart faileth: but
God is the strength of my heart, and my portion forever"
(Ps. 73:26).

This also points up a common mistake about Christ. I
know some sincere believers who say that to be a Christian you must repent, believe, be baptized, take the
Lord's Supper each Sunday, and refrain from drinking,
gambling, chewing tobacco, and watching anything on
television except Lawrence Welk. They make God nothing more than a lawgiver or a judge. And they almost
completely shut out the concept of a personal, loving,
caring Christ. They would say, "The Word became law
and judged among us," or "The Word became words and
spoke to us," but the Scripture asserts: "The Word was
made flesh, and dwelt among us" (John 1:14). He is still

dwelling among us. That is the work of the Holy Spirit —to make us know Christ in a personal way. When this relationship is achieved, true morality is lived out. No longer is it "I won't drink; I won't do drugs; I won't get hooked on sex; I won't gamble—because it is the law." Now it is a matter of loving him so much you would not do anything that would embarrass or hurt him, and your joy in him is so great you just don't need the world's empty kicks.

When they asked Christ what the greatest command-ment was, what did he say? "Thou shalt believe the Lord thy Word"? "Thou shalt reverence the Lord thy Law"? No. "Thou shalt love the Lord thy God with all thy heart, and with all thy soul, and with all thy strength, and with all thy mind" (Luke 10:27).

We all know the expressions on our faces and the lift in our hearts depend a great deal upon the company we are in. Within one group we look down, but let certain per-sons come into our view and see how our faces light up!

A real, loving relationship with God can do that for you. It can introduce you to a spiritual companionship that transfigures even the way you look. "I am not alone," you can know, "my Lord is with me." We can choose our inner, spiritual company. In that brief state-ment lies a truth that could remake our lives. Many things in the outer world you cannot choose. There we are victims of necessity, and during these days we often have to live in depressing company. But, within our-selves, we can choose our spiritual companionship.

When you have a personal, loving relationship with him, you will have whatever strength any hour de-mands. Life's most successful people are those whose hearts are filled with love for God. When you love him and his love lives in you, then my friend you have what it takes!

William R. Featherstone penned the words to a song that should be the affirmation of every Christian:

My Jesus, I love Thee, I know Thou art mine,
For Thee all the follies of sin I resign;
My gracious Redeemer, my Saviour art Thou;
If ever I loved Thee, my Jesus, 'tis now.

I love Thee because Thou hast first loved me,
And purchased my pardon on Calvary's tree;
I love Thee for wearing the thorns on Thy brow;
If ever I loved Thee, my Jesus, 'tis now.

I'll love Thee in life, I will love Thee in death,
And praise Thee as long as Thou lendest me breath;
And say when the death dew lies cold on my brow,
If ever I loved Thee, my Jesus, 'tis now.

In mansions of glory and endless delight
I'll ever adore Thee in heaven so bright;
I'll sing with the glittering crown on my brow,
If ever I loved Thee, my Jesus, 'tis now.[1]

Note

1. From *The Baptist Hymnal* © 1956, p. 289.

18

On the Other Side of Tragedy
2 Corinthians 4:8-9

How does a Christian face tragedy? On one side of the road of truth is the ditch of despair. On the other side is the opposite extreme, a sickly pseudospiritual "Pollyannishness" which pretends the hurt is not there. What is the truth about handling tragedy?

That Easter week in 1979 hadn't been a happy week. A flood, a creeping quiet monster, had stolen homes, furnishings, and businesses of many—the lives of some. A distraught man wrote from New Jersey, telling me his wife had deserted him. We lost one of our best men to a heart attack.

For twenty-five years, I've watched people handle life's hurts. Being a pastor demands that you go where hurt hits. When you've stood beside hurt in hospitals and funeral homes; when you've watched businesses fall, homes burn to the ground or fill up with water; when you've been with people who've lost those they love most in this world to death, or even worse sometimes, to moral failure, you begin to see it. It's a quality that always shows itself among God's people. It's that indispensable something that won't quit.

Standing with people waist deep in dirty water, in their own homes, you see it. One person said: "You despair, you cry when no one is looking if you can, but one of the things you're crying about is your loss of privacy. Even through the hurt you begin to notice it in yourself, 'Hey, I'm stronger than I thought.' I always had a sneaking suspicion I was sold out to life's furniture, the stuff. It hurts; we'll miss it; but we'll get it back. I know now I'm stronger that I thought. That's a good thing to know about yourself."

It's one of those Dale Carnegie type thoughts which,

at first, sounds sort of silly. Yet it is one of life's titanic truths. It is a truth which many of you have demonstrated in days past: "Attitudes are more important than facts. What happens to you is not nearly so important as how you take it."

The apostle Paul is Exhibit A. Whenever a door slammed in his face, he looked for a window. He had a God-given desire to preach the gospel to the world. Confidently he set out to do so. Imagine his bewilderment on the occasion of his first imprisonment. He had the world in his heart, yet he was confined to four bleak walls. From these experiences, when all he could do was write, has come much of the Word of God which is still reaching the world.

Paul and Silas were falsely arrested, beaten, and bound in a rough Roman prison (Acts 16). The facts of that situation were cruel and unjust, but their faith was courageous. Their attitude of commitment and praise turned a raw deal into a revival. From another prison Paul wrote to his friends in Philippi: "Now I want you to know, brethren, that my circumstances have turned out for the greater progress of the gospel" (Phil. 1:12, NASB).

The faith of a Daniel is that which transforms lions' dens into living rooms. The faith of Shadrach, Meshach, and Abed-nego is what takes the heat out of any of life's fires.

When life hits hard, remember this: There is a vast difference between bending and breaking. Don't entertain for a moment the Pollyannish idea that people of great faith don't get discouraged. Of course they do. Their faith is, that though God may allow them to be bent, he will never let them break. Listen to Paul in 2 Corinthians 4:8-9, "We are afflicted in every way, but not crushed; perplexed, but not despairing; persecuted, but not forsaken; struck down, but not destroyed" (NASB).

In Atlanta one year, a visitor to the opera mistook the intermission for the end of the program. While gathering hat and coat, he began to comment on the quality of the opera. How embarrassed he was to learn he'd only seen half the program and the grand finale was yet to come. Victorious people have learned that life isn't over just because the curtain comes down. After the intermission it starts again. Those who have learned to face the hard intermissions of life with hope have discovered this two-pronged truth: Most success is found on the far side of failure; triumph is waiting on the other side of tragedy.

The president of IBM was asked by a young man: "How can I succeed?"

"It's quite simple, really. Double your rate of failure."

Never before had Arthur Gordon heard advice like that. So, numbed by the statement, he just stared.

"You're making a common mistake," continued Mr. Watson. "You're thinking of failure as an enemy of success, but it isn't at all. Failure is a teacher, a harsh one perhaps, but the best. You can be discouraged by failure or you can learn from it. Remember, that's where you'll find success—on the far side of failure."[1]

Paul's testimony was of a man who tried hard to be a righteous man and failed. Through his failure, he came to Christ and spiritual success.

My wife and I sat in the pastor's study of Riverside Church, in New York City. That was the study built for Harry Emerson Fosdick, a preacher who pioneered and excelled in a form of preaching which applied the truths of God's Word to life's killing stresses—those inner conflicts which destroy people. You see, Dr. Fosdick, as a young man, had suffered a nervous breakdown. Through the agony of his own experience, he learned the truths he taught. His success was found on the far side of failure.

Benjamin Franklin sailed for London to purchase articles needed to set up a printing business. He had been promised the funds for this venture would be waiting for him there. They were not. He had been deceived. For eighteen months he worked to earn his passage back. During that time he gained valuable experience which helped make him a better printer and a better man.

Abraham Lincoln failed at almost every venture until he was elected president. He learned from his failure and found success. Babe Ruth struck out twice as many times as he hit home runs, but he kept swinging the bat and is remembered for his home runs. J. C. Penney lost everything in the great Chicago fire, but he rebuilt and found his success on the far side of failure.

The author of *Gone with the Wind*, Margaret Mitchell, was turned down by seven publishers who thought the novel had no commercial value. Had she not tried the eighth time we would never have heard of the novel that made her famous.

I am convinced that in a few years some who lost everything except good health and the moral support of loved ones will become a huge success because of the flood I mentioned earlier. They will have discovered in themselves amazing strength and determination, and it will carry them higher than they dreamed.

Study the biography of every person the world calls great. Survey the heroes of the Word of God. Almost without exception every success was on the far side of failure, and every triumph was on the other side of tragedy.

Life had tumbled in on William Cowper. At his lowest moment of despair, he hailed a cab to take him to the river. He considered every aspect of his life to be useless and hopeless. To end it all seemed the best way out. In the dense London fog the cab driver had difficulty finding the river. For more than an hour they drove through the fog. Angry at the driver for not getting him where he wanted to be, Cowper flung open the door of the cab. Imagine his surprise to find he was right back at his own doorstep. Stricken by so startling a coincidence he rushed inside and penned the lines that have cheered millions who have come to the brink of disaster:

Light Shining Out of Darkness

God works in a mysterious way,
   His wonders to perform;
He plants His footsteps in the sea,
   And rides upon the storm.

Deep in unfathomable mines
   Of never-failing skill,
He treasures up His bright designs,
   And works His sovereign will.

Ye fearful saints, fresh courage take;
   The clouds you so much dread
Are big with mercy and shall break
   In blessings on your head.

Judge not the Lord by feeble sense.
   But trust Him for His grace;
Behind a frowning providence,
   He hides a smiling face.

His purposes will ripen fast,
   Unfolding every hour;
The bud may have a bitter taste,
   But sweet will be the flower.

Blind unbelief is sure to err,
   And scan His work in vain;
God is His own interpreter,
   And He will make it plain.[2]

How does a Christian face tragedy, knowing that the road of God's truth is flanked on one side by the ditch of despair, and on the other side by the opposite extreme—a sickly pseudospiritual "Pollyannishness" which pretends the hurt is not there? A Christian faces discouragement with this attitude: "We are troubled on every side, yet not distressed; we are perplexed, yet not in despair; . . . cast down, but not destroyed" (2 Cor. 4:8-9). This is a faith that understands that attitudes are more important than facts; that what happens to you is not nearly so critical as how you take it; that success is almost always found on the far side of failure; and, that lasting triumph is waiting on the other side of tragedy.

Notes

1. Arthur Gordon, *A Touch of Wonder* (Old Tappan, New Jersey: Fleming Revell, 1974), p. 73.

2. *A Treasury of Religious Verse*, comp. Donald T. Koffman (New Jersey: Fleming Revell, 1962), p. 185.

19

My God . . . Why?

You can half jokingly call a place "Godforsaken." But what do you do when you feel Godforsakenness is not a location, but a personal condition; not the place you live, but the way you feel?

The place I was born and our family lived my first twelve years was a long way out in the country. In fact, it was located a mile from the dirt road! It wasn't a pretty place. It was never listed on the Garden Club's "Parade of Homes." We are the only people ever to live in that canyon. My family was the first to move in, and when we moved out, no one took our place. It's been thirty-five years, and still no one lives there. My mother had a name for it. In the South, people name their homes, like "Tara" in *Gone with the Wind*, or "The Hermitage," the home of Andrew Jackson. My mother called our place "Godforsaken." It means abandoned by God.

You can half jokingly call a place "Godforsaken," but what do you do when you feel Godforsakenness is not a location, but a personal condition; not the place you live, but the way you feel?

Probably the darkest dark I have experienced was in that canyon. There was no electricity there. There were no neighbors close enough to see their lights at night. It was dark. As a little boy, I walked out into that dark many a time with my dad, but I never wanted to go without him. It was just too dark to go out there without a father! You can walk into any dark when you know your Father is with you. But what if you don't feel his presence? You probably know what it is to be in some pit of despair and feel so alone—Godforsaken.

David felt it. Hear his cry of anguish in Psalm 22, beginning with verse 1:

My God, my God, why hast Thou forsaken me?
. . . .
O my God, I cry by day, but Thou dost not answer;
And by night, but I have no rest.
. . . .
But I am a worm, and not a man,
A reproach of men, and despised by the people.
All who see me sneer at me;
They separate with the lip, they wag the head,
    saying,
"Commit yourself to the Lord; let Him deliver him;
Let Him rescue him, because He delights in him."
(Ps. 22:1,2,6-8, NASB)

Christ also experienced it. For six hours, he hung on that cross in shameful, agonizing pain. For three hours it had been midnight dark at noonday. Now it was silent. Angels sang when he was born. Where was the music now? Out of the pain, the dark absence of life's music, came the words "My God, my God, why hast Thou forsaken Me?"

Does it bother you that Jesus said it? Do you join others who try to explain it away saying, "Perhaps he was speaking on behalf of those standing at the foot of the cross." This is part of his bearing your sins and mine. He took our place on the cross that day, and for you and me he went into the pit of despair. He felt Godforsaken, too.

As hard and harsh a feeling as that is for you and me, it was harder for him. He went into a much deeper despair. You and I have always had something standing between us and God. Our sins have always been there to rupture our relationship with him. There never had been anything between him and God. In Mark 9, we read of the Father splitting the heavens to say, "This is my beloved Son; hear him" (Mark 9:7). Jesus had told his peo-

ple, "I and my Father are one" (John 10:30). The night
before our Lord had prayed, "Father, as we are one, so I
pray that they may be one" (see John 17:21). Think how
hard it was on him to feel Godforsaken. If it is unbearable for you and me to think God's face is hidden, how
much more so for him. The pain of the nails was not
nearly so painful as the hurt of despair. He had suffered
the pain, the lies and insults of that mob. In his human
heart is the question: "Why doesn't my Father do something? Why does he let this happen? Where is my
Father?" When you have these feelings, remember he felt
it, too, and more than you and I ever will.

He felt it, too. Have you allowed that thought to really
grab your soul? He felt our temptations. Hebrews 4:15
declares that he "has been tempted in all things as we
are, yet without sin" (NASB).

Are you lonely? He felt that loneliness, too. There has
never been one in history as lonely and misunderstood as
Jesus Christ. Do you feel mistreated and abused? He felt
that, too. Look at that cross. Never in the history of the
world has there been a situation in which wrong was
more on the throne. He felt all of the despair you will
ever feel, for he felt cut off from God. In that moment, he
felt all the misery of hospital beds, deathbeds, battle-
fields, and personal failure. In that moment he felt all
the unbearable pain of being left alone, as if God had
turned his back on him.

There is a fellowship between people who have a common suffering. When someone can say, "I know, I've
been there, too," there is fellowship and comfort. Jesus
shares that fellowship with you.

Years ago the downtrodden, yet faith-filled, black
community sang: "Nobody knows the trouble I've seen.
Nobody knows, but Jesus." But, Jesus does know and
that makes all the difference in two worlds.

Joseph Parker, the gifted and noted preacher of New
York fame, suffered through the death of his wife. The

next Sunday morning he preached from this text: "My God, my God, why hast thou forsaken me?" And he said, "I'm so glad my Lord asked 'why' before me."

If you've ever lived on an unpaved road and had to be the first to drive on that road after a long, hard rain, you know how difficult that is. But how different it is if you are the second to drive on that road! You have some ruts to follow, and the going is better.

No matter what circumstances constitute the dark walls of your pit of despair, take heart in knowing that he knows. He felt it, too. But this is enough to say about his painful cry, "My God . . . why?" He was doing much more than identifying with our pain and despair. He was dying for you and me. He was dying, not because of his sins, but because of yours and mine. The cry "My God, my God, why hast thou forsaken me?" was the cry of the pain of God as he bore our sins and our sorrows.

No one around that day understood how serious their sins were, just as very few of you understand that sin is the most deadly and dreaded disease which can come upon a person. And we all have it. They gambled, taunted, and jeered that day while he was suffering more than anyone ever had, for them and us. From that great heart he prayed: "Father forgive them; for they do not know what they are doing" (Luke 23:34, NASB).

The Apostles' Creed speaks of Christ as "Died, dead, descended unto Hell." I hear people sometimes talk of "trying to get to God." Just the opposite is true. All through the years God has been trying to get to you. How far has he come? He has come all the way to hell. Hell is everything God's Word says it is, but the classic definition of hell is to be where God is not. When Christ cried, "My God, my God, why hast thou forsaken me?" he had gone all the way to hell to save us. Elizabeth C. Clephane captured some of this truth in her hymn "The Ninety and Nine." "But none of the ransomed ever knew/ How deep were the waters crossed;/Nor how dark was

the night that the Lord passed thro'/Ere He found His
sheep that was lost."

As is so often the case when we delve into the things of
God Almighty, we are dealing with a theological mystery
we shall never understand. When Christ cried: "My
God, my God, why hast thou forsaken me?" God was
turning his back upon himself. He was abandoning himself. He was losing himself in order to win you and me
back to a right relationship. He went to the very pit of
hell so that you and I may not ever have to go.

Now in this statement of Christ we find him identifying with our despair. We know he is taking our sin's
punishment upon himself, but also he is showing us how
to go through despair and beyond despair into victory.

So often, in our deep hurt, we may be prone to ask
others why God has forsaken us. Not so for Christ. He
addresses this statement to his Father, in whom he had
not lost confidence and trust. "My God, my God, why
hast thou forsaken me?" Because his trust and confidence
was in the Father, he went all the way through that
agony to victory. Later he would say: "It is finished"
(John 19:30) and "Father, into your hands I commend
my spirit" (Luke 23:46). The psalmist did not end his
psalm in despair, either. "For He has not despised nor
abhorred the affliction of the afflicted; neither has He
hidden His face from him; but when he cried to Him for
help, He heard" (Psalm 22:24, NASB).

This is the message of this word from our Lord.
Through Christ, you can come all the way through despair. You don't have to stay there. If he had only hurt as
we hurt, it would be a small victory. But, he emerged on
the other side.

Experiencing this victory is a present reality. This cannot be restricted to the few hours of the gruesome pageantry of the cross. He is still with us. He is with you in
all your hurt and pain and despair. He is still suffering
because of our sin. He still bears the burden for your sins

and mine. Because he went all the way to that hell and out of it, there is life for you and me.

Maybe you've heard before in this setting the story of George Frederick Handel. As a young musician, he was suffering in every sense of the word. He was famous. He played before royalty. He received the applause of men. Yet, because of professional jealousy, all this was taken away from him and his career came to a halt. Then he suffered a stroke at a young age and was left half-paralyzed. After long months of suffering, he emerged a beaten man.

They say he walked the streets of London without a penny in his pocket. Witnesses claim that as he roamed the streets he was heard to say: "My God, my God, why hast Thou forsaken me?"

One day he returned to his little dirty room and found a packet. Someone had left some words which they wanted him to put to music. For twenty-four days he was totally consumed in this project. At the end of those days George Frederick Handel had written the *Messiah*. As he wrote the *Messiah* he knew, because he had been there, what it was to be despised and rejected. And he came into a larger fellowship, for he was not despised alone. He knew he was not in despair alone. These truths took hold of his bones and out of it came the music that shakes our souls when we hear it:

> Hallelujah!
> Hallelujah!
> For the Lord God omnipotent reigneth.
> Hallelujah!
> Hallelujah!
> The kingdom of this world is become the kingdom of
>   our Lord Christ.
> And He shall reign forever and ever. King of kings
>   and Lord of lords.
> Hallelujah!

Hallelujah!
And He shall reign forever and ever!

"Thanks be to God, who gives us the victory through our Lord Jesus Christ" (1 Cor. 15:57, NASB). My friend, because Jesus Christ went all the way through the hell of despair, you don't have to!

20

On Being One Person, Undivided
Genesis 39:1-6

The most beautiful thing about God's revelation is the way he dresses his truth in personality. In twelve chapters of Genesis he outlines, in unmistakable clarity, what integrity looks like. Integrity lived in a man named Joseph.

If it fell your lot to choose a person to fill the most important position of leadership in your land, what kind of person would you look for? If somehow it became your responsibility to be that person, what characteristic or what personal character trait would you pray for?

I think the word to describe what would be needed is *integrity*. "Basically the word means wholeness. In mathematics, an integer is a number that isn't divided into fractions. Just so, a man of integrity isn't divided against himself. He doesn't think one thing and say another, so it's virtually impossible for him to lie. He doesn't believe one thing and do another, so he's not in conflict with his own principles. It's the absence of inner warfare . . ." that gives one extra energy and clarity of thought.[1]

The most beautiful thing about God's revelation is the wonderful way he dresses his truth in personality. In twelve chapters of Genesis he outlines, with unmistakable clarity, what integrity looks like. Integrity lived in a man named Joseph whom God used to save several nations from starvation.

Joseph, like many great men, did not have an impressive family background. His grandfather, Laban, and his father, Jacob, were known as the slickest dealers in the East. Neither was a man you'd want to buy a used camel from. Joseph watched the relationship between his father and grandfather totally deteriorate. He experienced that stressful flight in which his father was running from the anger of Laban straight into a confrontation with Esau, a brother he had cheated. Esau had made a vow to kill Jacob. Perhaps in the context of that dilemma, seeing what problems his father's trickery had caused, Joseph decided that honesty is the best policy—maybe the only one, if you want to survive.

There were some positive experiences on that trip. Joseph watched his father come back from a midnight encounter with God. He walked with a limp, but he was changed in other ways, too. He was humble, strong, and confident. He had been changed by the living God.

Joseph saw another wonderful thing on that trip. He saw his uncle, Esau, do a totally unexpected, unnatural thing. He welcomed, accepted, and forgave the brother who had cheated him out of his birthright. In Genesis 33, we read of the meeting of these two brothers. Esau said, in effect: "I don't want any revenge. I don't want you to make amends, nor do I want any of your goods. I just want to be your brother."

In verse 10, Jacob said: "Esau, your face looks to me like the face of God" (author's paraphrase). How could the face of old, hairy Esau look like God's face? It was the face of love and forgiveness, and that does look like the face of God! I'm sure little Joseph never forgot that confrontation.

At seventeen, Joseph was spoiled rotten and arrogant. He was obviously favored by his father. He flaunted that relationship before his other brothers and angered the whole family by telling of dreams in which they all bowed down to worship him. And he ran to his father with news of every bad thing he saw his brothers doing. None of the above endeared him to those brothers. At the first opportunity, they rid themselves of Joseph by selling him as a slave to some Egyptian merchants.

Thus, at seventeen, Joseph faced the cruel test of adversity. He was separated from his father, his security. He was now a slave. In Egypt he was sold to a man named Potiphar. Yet, even in slavery, he prospered. After ten years, he was the trusted steward, the manager, of all of Potiphar's property.

Having weathered well this first test of adversity, he now faced the test of allurement. By now, Joseph was twenty-seven years old. Genesis 39:6 states he was "handsome in form and appearance." These attributes of this Hebrew Robert Redford did not escape the lustful eye of Mrs. Potiphar. The sin she suggested was not all that uncommon in Egyptian society. For ten years, Joseph had been away from any moral teaching. Yet he resisted day after day and steadfastly declared he could not betray his master or sin against his God.

For this he was tragically rewarded. The spurned woman spread lies, and soon Joseph found himself in prison. Some of God's great people have faced this kind of adversity. What a splendid opportunity to throw up your hands in despair or clinch your fist in resentment and ponder what kind of mad dog world this is which attacks the innocent. By God's grace, Paul and Silas, in a Philippian jail, turned a raw deal into a revival. In an even greater display of faith, Joseph weathered this trial for three years.

Then Joseph faced the biggest trial of all—the trial of success. Success has ruined more men than failure. Yet, Joseph handled that, too.

In a bizarre and divinely directed turn of events, Joseph was named Governor of Egypt—second in command to the Pharaoh. Genesis 41:43 tells us Joseph was given the chariot of the second-in-command, sort of an ancient Egyptian counterpart to Air Force Two, and wherever he went people were commanded to kneel down.

Joseph handled his advancement well. The time eventually came when his brothers were totally at his mercy. He could have done with them anything he pleased, but his forgiving spirit was like that of Esau's years before.

Joseph was lied about and hated, yet he did not return lies or resort to hating. He dreamed big dreams, yet was not destroyed when life seemed headed in another direction. He faced the greatest disaster and the highest triumph and did not lose his integrity to either.

Joseph lived up to the best in himself. Many are the people who ignore the best in themselves and surrender to the worst in themselves.

He had a highly developed sense of honor. He knew that some things are forever right and some things are forever wrong—no matter if you are in Egypt. He had a conscience and listened to it. Instead of suppressing his conscience, he obeyed it. That made him a powerful man.

Joseph also had the courage of his convictions. There is no more powerful person to be found than one who knows he is right. Someone has observed that those who ultimately succeed, those whose lives make a difference, are those who are driven by an "obedience to the unenforceable." They do right no matter what others do. They do more than they are expected to.

Would you like to be a person of integrity—a whole person, undivided? You can. The secret is spelled out four times in Genesis 39. Look at verse two: "And the Lord was with Joseph"; verse three: "Now his master saw that the Lord was with him"; verse twenty-one, "But the Lord was with Joseph"; and the last half of verse 23, "because the Lord was with him" (NASB).

Do you want to be a whole person? Come to God through faith in Jesus Christ, and the Lord will be with you. In fact, he says, "I will never leave thee, nor forsake thee" (Heb. 13:5).

We need people of integrity today. Do you want to do

the best thing for your country? Don't criticize the president; become a better person! Let Jesus Christ live and rule your life. He'll put it all together and you'll be one person, *undivided*.

Note

1. Arthur Gordon, *A Touch of Wonder* (Old Tappan, New Jersey: Fleming Revell, 1974), p. 225.

21

Forgive Yourself
Matthew 18:21-35

You may think the church is more a "guilt center" than a "forgiveness center." How many professing Christians are preoccupied with guilt? You carry it around all the time. Your guilt robs you of so much, and it robs others of what you could give them. The one thing that keeps most of us from our Father's business is preoccupation with our guilt.

We hear the word *center* a lot. First it was the shopping center. Now there are sewing centers, food centers, and entertainment centers. Some churches, disdaining the stuffy connotations of the word *sanctuary*, call the place of worship the worship center.

I think churches ought to be known as forgiveness centers. The New Testament describes churches as a family of the loved and the loving, the forgiven and the forgiving. It is in Christ that you find forgiveness. It is in Christ that you become a forgiving person.

Jesus never said: "I am come that you might have guilt and have it more abundantly." He said in John 10:10, "I am come that they might have life, and that they might have it more abundantly."

You may think the church is more a guilt center than a forgiveness center. How many professional Christians are preoccupied with guilt? You carry it around all the time. Your guilt robs you of so much, and it robs others of what you could give them. The one thing that keeps most of us from our Father's business is preoccupation with our guilt.

Guilt isn't something that can be denied, and it will vanish. You may sear your conscience, but it's like varnishing rotten wood or painting over rust. You may cover it up for a while, but the problem is still there.

In a moment of reality, a wise friend may counsel: "You must forgive yourself; you must accept yourself."

You reply: "You're right. I know it, but how do I do it?"
The friend says: "You must do it!" You say "How?" And
the wise friend is silent, but the Word of God is vocal!

To the vital issue four questions are posed. First:
"Have you accepted Jesus Christ as Savior and Lord?"
Second: "Are you majoring on your guilt or his grace?"
Third: "Can you forgive others?" And fourth: "Can you
forgive yourself?"

Inscribe this indelibly in your mind and heart. You
cannot be free from guilt unless Jesus Christ is your Lord.
I am not asking you to try to begin living a Christian life.
You can't do it. I'm asking you to confess your sinfulness
to God and admit your total lack of power to save yourself and to receive by faith the forgiveness which comes
only through Jesus Christ. He said: "I am the way, and
the truth, and the life; no one comes to the Father, but
through Me" (John 14:6, NASB).

A non-Christian is separated from God by true moral
guilt. If you aren't a Christian, you feel guilty because
you are guilty. The Bible declares in Romans 3:23 that
we are all sinners, both by mistake and by intention.
This true guilt is removed only by the Christ who took
our sins upon himself on the cross and became the sacrificial Lamb of God.

Our guilt is removed only on the basis of the finished
work of Christ plus nothing on our part. There must be
no humanistic note added at any point in our accepting
the gospel. Ephesians 2:8-9 declares: "For by grace you
have been saved [an accomplished fact] through faith;
and that not of yourselves, it is the gift of God; not as a
result of works, that no one should boast" (NASB).

When we come believing God and accepting Christ's
sacrifice on the cross as full payment for our sins, the
Bible asserts we are justified by God; the guilt is gone!
The instrument for receiving this forgiveness is faith.
This is not faith in faith. It isn't a leap in the dark. It's
faith in the specific promises of God.

When you lift up empty hands of faith and accept the

finished work of Christ on the cross, you are passed from death into life. This is what it means to be born again. This is the first step, the most indispensable step in learning to forgive yourself. You can never feel forgiven till you are forgiven.

The next question is: "Are you majoring on your guilt or his grace? Do you think more of how bad you are or how good he is?"

In the middle 1950s some seminary students noticed that many of the people who spoke in chapel were converted gangsters, murderers, drug addicts, and others whose life-styles hadn't been recommended in the Sunday School quarterly. Each spelled out in sensational detail his sorry past and ended by telling how he had become a Christian. One morning there appeared on the most prominent bulletin board on campus a giant poster, headed: "How To Be A Great Evangelist!" Listed were statements like: "Be an ex-convict"; "Be an ex-murderer"; "Be an ex-drug addict." At the end of the last statement there was an asterisk. It guided you to another asterisk by some tiny lettering at the bottom which read: "If you have none of these requirements, we suggest you take two years off and establish your background."

This was not to discredit the work of God's grace in those lives, but to point out that the biblical emphasis is upon his grace—not in the detailing of our sins. Christians are to exalt Christ, not parade our past sins.

We've never read in Holy Writ of David saying:

> I committed murder and adultery. Now my whole household is in rebellion. My own sons are fighting me. One of my sons raped my daughter. You should have seen me in the good old days when I was God's man.

We don't read that in the Scriptures. We read of David saying: "I have sinned against the Lord" (2 Sam. 12:13, NASB). We hear Nathan reply: "The Lord also has taken away your sin." Then David resumes his life as God's man.

Can you imagine a first-century gathering? The pastor announces: "Have we got an exciting testimony for you tonight! I want you to meet Brother Paul. He'll tell you what an awful man he's been!"

Paul gets up and rehearses it again. He tells them how bad he's been: how he murdered Christians and plundered the church; how many people were misled by his intellect, his teaching, and his denial of Jesus Christ. While that story is in Acts as a part of the church's history, it wasn't the main topic of Paul's message. It wasn't his preoccupation. He didn't waste his time, or others', by posing as the hero of his own sins. Rather, he exalted Christ as the hero of his forgiveness.

The main thrust of his message is found in 2 Corinthians 5:17,

> Therefore if any man is in Christ, he is a new creature [new creation]; the old things passed away [no matter how bad or horrible, or how many people were involved]; behold, new things have come [the world, its people, and myself have become new] (NASB).

Paul exalted Christ rather than wallowing in the garbage of his life, which had already been dumped in the sea of God's forgetfulness. On almost every page of Holy Writ, Christians are commanded to dwell in the high places of praise and gratitude to him for his grace. What a shame that so many unnecessarily wallow in the garbage dump of their past sins.

Listen anew to what Paul says in Philippians 3:13-14, "forgetting what lies behind and reaching forward to what lies ahead, I press on toward the goal for the prize of the upward call of God in Christ Jesus" (NASB).

This is the secret of a forgiving heart. If you'll stop

magnifying your guilt, you'll stop magnifying the guilt of others. The Bible says: "For he thinketh in his heart, so is he." Someone paraphrased it: "You become what you think about all day." If you "turn your eyes upon Jesus," think about his forgiving grace and praise him for it, then you become more like him. That forgiving grace not only works in you, but also works through you.

Thus the next question: "Can you forgive others?" In Matthew 6:9-13, Christ teaches us a model prayer. One line declares: "And forgive us our debts, as we also have forgiven our debtors" (v. 12, NASB). This is the only part of the prayer that Jesus chose to explain in greater detail. Immediately after the "Amen," he said: "For if you forgive men for their transgressions, your heavenly Father will also forgive you. But if you do not forgive men, then your Father will not forgive your transgressions" (vv. 14-15, NASB).

In many different ways, our Lord lays this heavy truth upon us. In Matthew 18:21-35, we find Simon Peter asking Christ, in effect, "How much do we have to take? How many times do we have to forgive someone? Is seven times enough?" Jesus answered: "Not just seven times, but seventy times seven." I don't think our Lord meant that on the 491st time Peter could clobber someone instead of forgiving him. He was asking, "How many times has God forgiven you?"

Then he told a story of a man who owed someone a greater fortune than Palestine's national budget. It was a debt so staggering he could never hope of repaying it. When payment was due, he begged for mercy and amazingly received it! In one minute he was under the burden of an unimaginable debt. Then, he was forgiven the debt. By an unbelievable grace the debt was stamped "Paid In Full," though he had not paid one penny. After this experience the forgiven man confronted someone who owed him twenty dollars. He rejected his debtor's pleas for mercy and had him thrown in jail. When the

word got back to his benefactor he called the man in and
said: "You are wicked! How could you receive multiplied
millions of dollars worth of forgiveness and not forgive a
twenty dollar debt?"

This application is readily apparent. All of us who
know Jesus deserve hell, yet have been given heaven. Our
sins deserve punishment, yet we've been given free pardon. How can we who know God's great love not forgive
when he has said to all who have sinned: "Neither do I
condemn you" (John 8:11, NASB). When we know the
truth from Romans 8:1, "There is therefore now no con-
demnation for those who are in Christ Jesus," (NASB), then
how can we condemn others?

But you may say, "Wait a minute, Preacher! This
chapter is entitled 'Forgive Yourself.' You've talked about
God forgiving us and our forgiving others, but you've not
yet addressed the main topic." Friend, these four questions are progressive. You must answer a positive "yes" to
each one, in order, before you answer the next.

The first question is, "Is Christ your Savior?" Have
you come to him, confessing your sinfulness and asking
his forgiveness, knowing his death on the cross is full and
complete payment for your sin? Guilt will gnaw on you
in life and consume you in eternity unless you receive him
as your Savior.

Secondly, if you are forgiven, are you living like a forgiven person? Do you praise him and make him the hero
of your forgiveness? No matter what you've done, no
matter how much water has gone over the dam, he owns
the dam and he owns the water. Praise him for his love
and grace. If you have been forgiven and you live like a
forgiven person, then you will be a forgiving person.
When you are a forgiving person, then you can even forgive yourself. When this happens you have learned, and
can joyfully share, the liberating experience of being
saved by the grace of God!

22

The Power of Purpose
Genesis 28

Do you realize happiness is essentially a state of going somewhere, wholeheartedly and unidirectionally, without regret or reservation?

Let me ask you, "If you get where you are going, where are you going to be?" Do you realize that happiness is essentially a state of going somewhere wholeheartedly, unidirectionally, without regret or reservation? The day you determine the direction your life will take is a life-changing day. It can happen when you are fifteen, fifty, or eighty, but it will change your life. Listen to the account of how intelligent, ambitious, sharp young Jacob had an experience which brought direction and power to his life.

Jacob had one of those experiences that I think, in one degree or another, we all have at times in life (Gen. 28). He experienced the presence of God and felt something wonderful because of it. But the difference was that the next morning when the experience was over, he didn't walk away from it or put it out of his mind. He determined that he would do something. Let's begin reading in Genesis 28: 18:

> So Jacob rose early in the morning, and took the stone that he had put under his head and set it up as a pillar, and poured oil on its top. And he called the name of that place Bethel; however, previously the name of the city had been Luz. Then Jacob made a vow, saying, "If God will be with me and will keep me on this journey that I take, and will give me food to eat and garments to wear, and I return to my father's house in saftey, then the Lord will be my

God. And this stone, which I have set up as a pillar,
will be God's house; and of all that Thou dost give
me I will surely give a tenth to Thee" (Gen.
28:18-22, NASB).

From that day forward, Jacob became a powerful
individual because his life had the power of purpose. Do
you want to be a powerful person? You can. You need to
have your life focused around a purpose. When that purpose is God's purpose, then you have all the power of the
universe at your disposal.

George Truett once said:

> Everyone should have a work to do and know what
> it is and do it with all his might. Decision is energy;
> energy is power; power is confidence; and confi-
> dence, to a remarkable degree, contributes to suc-
> cess. Many a man has failed not from lack of abil-
> ity, but from lack of this element of concentration.

One businessman said, "The way to succeed is to put
all your eggs in one basket and watch that basket." With
that in mind, read what Paul says in Philippians 3, beginning with verse 12:

> Not that I have already obtained it, or have already
> become perfect, but I press on in order that I may
> lay hold of that for which also I was laid hold of by
> Christ Jesus. Brethren, I do not regard myself as
> having laid hold of it yet, but one thing I do: forget-
> ting what lies behind and reaching forward to what
> lies ahead, I press on toward the goal for the prize of
> the upward call of God in Christ Jesus (Phil.
> 3:12-14, NASB).

How can you experience the power of this kind of commitment? Well, of course, the first thing is you need to
accept Jesus Christ as your Savior and Lord and become

a disciple, a follower of Jesus Christ. And then there are three statements that every Christian, I think, ought to make, and spiritual help is involved in these three statements.

The first: I will not stop growing.

The second: I will not be ruled by the past.

The third: I will meet the challenge of God's will.

Every Christian ought to say, "I will not stop growing. I will keep on becoming what he would have me be." A Christian must never consider himself full-grown. When a fellow says, "I know all I need to know; I am all I need to be; I am spiritually full-grown; I am satisfied with myself," then look out! Satan has that person going his way.

In the booklet, *Witness Take the Stand,* there are some questions designed to awaken Christianity's Rip Van Winkles. Ponder the past twelve months of your Christian life and ask yourself: Have you obviously matured spiritually? Is your prayer life more meaningful? Do you pray without ceasing? Does Christ use more of you now to witness and to love?

Consider the ten people closest to your life. What evaluation of your faith would they make as a result of being associated with you? How we Christians need to continue growing! This world is full of people who got older, but never grew up. We all need to grow.

Growth is a natural process, isn't it? One day our Lord pointed to the wild lilies growing on a Palestinian hillside and said, "Consider the lilies, . . . how they grow," (Matt. 6:28). How do they grow? Well, they grow spontaneously, organically, and automatically without struggling or fretting. And that's how a child grows up physically. He can stretch himself and say, "I'm going to make myself tall," but this effort does not make him a fraction taller. Jesus asked, "Which of you by taking thought can add one cubit unto his stature?" (Matt. 6:27). When a child grows it has to be like Topsy. She just grows and grows.

The same is true of a Christian. When you receive Christ, you start out as a spiritual baby. "As newborn babes, desire the sincere milk of the word, that ye may grow thereby," says 1 Peter 2:2. Yet there are things that nurture and help growth. For the plant there must be good soil, moisture, and the right climate. For the child, there must be good food, exercise, and proper rest to help him grow. Without these things the child will not grow.

For the Christian to grow, he must have three things. It is important that you build up your soul by reading the Scripture. 1 Peter 2:2 calls the Word "the milk that helps us grow." In Psalm 119:9 the question is asked, "How can a young man keep his way pure?" The answer: "By keeping it according to Thy word" (NASB). Verse 11 reads: "Thy word have I hid in my heart, that I might not sin against Thee." Satan will do anything to keep you from reading God's Word.

A growing Christian must learn to pray. Jesus said men ought always to pray. Prayer is talking to God. The more you talk to him, the better you will be at it.

A rancher in Wichita Falls became a Christian late in his life. Just a few years ago, at a morning service during a revival, someone called on him to pray. He had never been asked to do a thing like that before. He bowed his head and said, "Lord, we ain't had any public dealings before, but you know that I love you."

One of the greatest prayers a new Christian could pray is to begin the day saying, "Lord, thank you for saving me. I love you. I am available for your use today. In Jesus' name, Amen."

If a Christian is to grow, he must have fellowship with other Christians. This means you will be active in a church. In Hebrews 10, we are admonished not to forsake the assembling of ourselves together. Friend, there is no way that television can take the place of church and don't you let that happen. When a coal is removed from the rest of the fire, it becomes cold. When a Christian is removed from other Christians in the fellowship of a church, he becomes cold and loses his warmth and growth. It is for this reason that Satan will find fault with everything and everyone in the church to try to convince Christians to stay away.

A Christian will not only be determined to grow, but he will not be ruled by his past. You must say, "I will not be ruled by my past." Paul said he was "forgetting those things which are behind" (Phil. 3:13). Remember these words are from Paul, the man whose past had included the great persecution of Christians and also great victories for Christ. He could have dwelt on his past mistakes and been miserable, or he could have pondered the pleasant pictures of past victories, but he chose not to be held down by either. We must do the same. Today is the vital issue. The important thing is not how well you used to do or how poorly you used to do, but what you will do now.

There are three complexes a Christian must watch. There is the "has been" complex. The church of Jesus Christ is filled with "Wizards of Was"—folks who forget that loving and serving God is always in the present, active tense. Equally damaging is the "has not been" complex. This is the one that says "I'm a failure. I not only am a 'has not been,' I'm a 'never will be.' I couldn't do it, can't do it, and won't be able to do it." Now each of these expressions is only an opinion, an expression of a defeated heart. Dedicate yourself to God and ask him to use you, and he will.

I suppose the most damaging poison that imprisons a Christian to his past is a guilt complex. If the apostle Paul spent much time thinking about his past sins, he would not have been a great servant of God. It is so with us all. The Bible says that God forgives and forgets our sins when we turn from them and ask his forgiveness. In Jeremiah 31:34 our Lord promises, "I will forgive their iniquity, and I will remember their sin no more."

In Hebrews 8:12 we read, "For I will be merciful to their unrighteousness, and their sins and their iniquities will I remember no more." To dwell on past sins is to invite one of two things: thinking about it will lead you to sin again, or you will spend your time in self-destructing despair. God has placed our sins in the sea of his forgetfulness and has put up a sign: "No Fishing Here."

If you can learn to forgive yourself as God forgives you, then you can become a most useful Christian—"forgetting those things which are behind." The other thing you need to say is, "I will meet the challenge of God's will." A Christian wants to do God's will. "But I press on in order that I may lay hold of that for which also I was laid hold of by Christ Jesus" (NASB). This is a titanic thought. He is saying, "When I was saved, Jesus had a dream for me, an ideal for me to fulfill. He had something in mind he wanted me to become. I want to grab hold of that dream and fulfill it." This is true for all of us. Our Lord saves us to bless us and use us. He has a dream, a plan for us, and we want to fulfill it.

A little bit of poetry written by Thomas S. Jones, Jr., entitled "Sometimes," states:

> Across the fields of yesterday
> He sometimes comes to me,
> A little lad just back from play—
> The lad I used to be.
> And yet he smiles so wistfully
> Once he has crept within,
> I wonder if he hopes to see
> The man I might have been.[1]

Upon reading these lines, I was struck by the thought that perhaps a part of judgment is to face the difference between what we are and what our Lord intended that we become. With a challenge to live for God's glory, not wanting to let him down or frustrate his great dream for our lives, we must say with Paul, "I will reach for that which is before. I press toward the mark."

"Reaching forth" in verse 13 comes from an athletic setting. It is the picture of a sprinter going hard for the tape. He is straining every muscle to get to the goal. His eyes are fixed on that finish line, and all the determination and dedication he has is aimed at winning that race.

May our Lord give each Christian the insight to say,

> Oh, Lord, I do want to fulfill your dream for my life. I don't want to let you down. Therefore, I will keep growing. I will not be pulled down by the past and I will meet the challenge of your goal for my life. From this day forth, "I am thine, oh Lord."

No